# LIFE...

## Though I Walked Through the Valley of the Shadow of Death

From Death Row to Life

**Sheaniqua Clarkson-Batty**

## LIFE, Though I Walked Through the Valley of the Shadow of DEATH
From Death Row to Life

Although the author and publisher have made every effort to ensure that the information in this book was correct at press time, the author and publisher (Sheaniqua Clarkson-Batty & Divine Purpose Publishing) do not assume and hereby disclaim any liability to any party for any loss, damage, or disruption caused by errors or omissions, whether such errors or omissions result from negligence, accident, or any other cause.

The names of certain individuals referenced in this publication have been changed. This publication contains the opinions and ideas of its author. Relevant laws vary from state to state. The strategies outlined in this book may not be suitable for every individual, and are not guaranteed or warranted to produce any particular results.

No warranty is made with respect to the accuracy or completeness of the information contained herein, and both the author and publisher specifically disclaim any responsibility for any liability, loss, or risk, personal or otherwise, which is incurred as a consequence, directly or indirectly, of the use and application of any of the contents of this book.

Scripture quotations marked KJV are from the KING JAMES VERSION of the Bible.

Published by DiViNE Purpose Publishing
www.divinepurposepublishing.com
P.O. Box 906
Branford, CT. 06405
(866) 211-7637 Ext. 0

ISBN-13: 978-0692487501
ISBN-10: 0692487506
LCCN: 2015910983

Printed in the United States of America

# DEDICATIONS

I am dedicating this book first and foremost to my Lord and Savior Jesus Christ, for he has graced me to live and tell my story. Jesus have given me life and made me everything that I am today. He created me, anointed me and ordained me for purpose. God saw the best in me, when I did not have the common sense, to see the best in myself. He covered me, washed me and made me whole with His blood. My past held me captive, but Jesus came and freed my mind, heart and soul from the handcuffs and shackles that held me bound. My Lord and Savior Jesus Christ reached out, grabbed me and pulled me out of my dry place (death) into the marvelous light (life). The Lord took my hand in marriage, knowing I would rejected Him. The Lord has been faithful to me, even though I have not always been faithful to Him. He has loved me unconditionally, even though my actions had shown otherwise. My Lord and Savior Jesus Christ have gone beyond the unimaginable for me, even though I am unworthy of it; and for this, I thank Him and dedicate this book to Him. I love you daddy (Jesus).

I am also dedicating this book to my mother and two sons for their understanding and support through the process of birthing this book forth. I bless God for you because you understood the sacrifice that it took in order to fulfill the assignment that is upon my life. I love you and I do not take it lightly that you are gifts from God. You have pushed me, encouraged me and stood with me through it all. I know that at times you did not understand the things that I went through in life; but I bless God that he gave you the heart to love me, strength to fight with me and the press to keep me lifted up before the Lord. I love you so much and I am so blessed to be apart of your lives. God bless you.

To those who spoke into my life what God spoke concerning writing this book, for it was confirmation on what God had already spoken to me many years ago. I thank you for the push that helped me birth this book. I love you all and may God continue to bless you.

Last, but most certainly not the least, I dedicate this book to the nations. This is for every male, woman and child. I dedicate this book to you. This is my gift to you. I gave you apart of my life to heal, deliver and set free. I gave you apart of my life to uproot, transform, renew, restore, revive and replenish the heart, mind and soul. I love you all and may God continue to bless you.

# CONTENTS

# PREFACE

*Life, Though I Walked through the Valley of the Shadow of Death* is a testimony of my real life story from birth through the age of 26 years old. The vision from God to write this book took consistent fasting and praying. The purpose of this book has been written to let you know that you are overcome by your testimony (Revelations 12:11) KJV. The events that took place in my life did not feel good nor did it look good at the time, but I had to go through it, because there was going to come a time that I would have to tell my story to heal, deliver and set free the souls of the nations. This is a Christian based book that have biblical scriptures quoted from the King James Version Bible throughout the contents of this book. This will lead, guide, equip and empower every man, woman and child of every nationality. There is a God who sits on high and look down low. He sees and hears all. He holds the world's Guinness Book of records for never losing a battle. He laid down His life paying off every debt from sin that we owed, so that we can live. The purpose of this book has been written to bring hope and comfort to the hurt and wounded. The purpose of this book will encourage you to look at the will be of your life, rather than the imperfections of the past and present. The purpose of this book has been written to minister to the souls that God appointed to do a great work for His Kingdom; but because of the handcuffs and shackles from the past, strongholds took root and unwanted situations called bricks, built walls. This book of my life story will show you how to have a Paul and Silas experience to break loose from handcuffs and shackles. This book of my life story will show you how to have an Israelite experience to tare down those walls of Jericho. This book will give you the faith and strength of the woman with the issue of blood to overcome what seems impossible. The mind is the devils battlefield and it is time to rebuke the tricks of the enemy. The enemy's job is to make you think that there is nothing else to do but accept defeat and die. I come to tell you, the devil is a liar and the truth is not in him. The rocky roads of life have prevented you from moving forward in Christ Jesus. Upon completing this book, you will know what to do when encountering the storm, what to do when going through the storm, how to go about making it out of the storm and now that you are out; where do you go from here. In order for healing and deliverance to manifest in your life, you must forgive yourself and others. Throughout the text of this book you will come across times when I speak in "Self Dialog." I want to speak to you one on one establishing a personal relationship with you through our Lord and Savior Jesus Christ. This will allow me to minister to you personally on all levels and then go back into my life story. Beware, that when you enter this book of healing, deliverance and freedom the Holy Spirit will consume you and transform you forever. The curses will be broken off of your life, strongholds cast down and freedom will reign in your life in Jesus name. Amen.

# CHAPTER ONE

## *The Valley of Generational Curses*

### *Spiritual Food for Thought*

**Mark 7:20-23** *states:* [20] *And he said, That which cometh out of the man, that defileth the man.* [21] *For from within, out of the heart of men, proceed evil thoughts, adulteries, fornication, murders,* [22] *Theft, covetousness, wickedness, deceit, lasciviousness, an evil eye, blasphemy, pride, foolishness:* [23] *All these evil things come from within and defile the man.*

### *Spiritual Food for Thought*

**Exodus 20:5-6** *states:* [5] *Thou shalt not bow down thyself to them, nor serve them: for I the LORD thy God am a jealous God, visiting the iniquity of the fathers upon the children unto the third and fourth generation of them that hate me;* [6] *And shewing mercy unto thousands of them that love me, and keep my commandments.*

# Self Dialog

Whatever our great grandparents, grandparents or parents did, the third and fourth generation can reap what has been sown. Have you ever heard of the phrase "You reap what you sow?" Reaping from sinful acts may not come back on the person who committed the sin, but it can carry on to the next generation leading to generational curses. In our daily living, we have to be careful because our actions or choices effect the people around us. If you sow well, then you will reap well. If you sow badly, then you will reap badly. Generational curses have been known as a dark cloud that travels from generation to generation. Generational curses is more like the phrase "Tag your it."

Repetitious sin that keep going and going until it becomes an inheritance. Whatever our ancestors did, somehow, some of us ended up embracing them good or bad. Generational curses appear as a normal everyday living. Whatever (great grandfather and great grandmother) did or allowed themselves to come in contact with can be inherited by their children, which is (grandfather and grandmother). Whatever (grandfather and grandmother) did or allowed themselves to come in contact with can be inherited by their children, which is (father and mother). Whatever (father and mother) did or allowed themselves to come in contact with can be inherited by their children, which is (you). Dealing with unclean spirits handicaps the inner man.

Have you ever wondered why people in your family are always mad for no reason? Have you ever wondered why the victim of molestation or rap runs through your family? Have you ever wondered why poverty run throughout your family? Have you ever wondered why family members pursue a vision, but somewhere along the way things get hindered or never get accomplished? Have you ever wondered why there are so many single parent households in your family? Have you ever wondered why so many of your family member suffer from alcohol and/or drug abuse? Have you ever wondered why certain illnesses such as cancer, diabetes and high blood pressure run throughout the family? There is no secret as to what is going on in your family. This is an inherited curse that has been passed down from generation to generation. Generational curses can arrive from sin. Yes, SIN because one likes what he or she does with no intentions on changing. When sin have a stronghold on someone, when conviction comes, one ignores it because it satisfies the flesh. Generational curses consist of issues such as emotional, physical, sexual and mental dysfunction. One generational curse that is so familiar from past to present among nations today is sexual immoralities, such as lust, fornication, adultery, masturbation, molestation, homosexuality, lesbianism, bestiality, swingers and pornography.

All of these sexual sins lead to emotional and mental issues. These are repeated cycles of sin causing strongholds. When a sinful act becomes a habit, one become immune to such acts. When one become immune to sin, the flesh began looking for something else to quench it because the flesh is no longer satisfied causing an emotional and mental disturbance. Emotional and mental issues come from dealing with demonic spirits called depression, isolation, guilt, rejection, negligence, fear and doubt. This is where the mind taps into serious warfare. Mental abuse is the devils play ground. The devil is on a mission to take the mind of Gods people but I come by way of the Holy Spirit to tell you that the devil is a liar!!! The devil will not and cannot have your mind, for it belongs to the Lord!!! I declare and decree that your mind is regulating even now and peace shall reside therein. I know a present help and his name is Jesus. The bible tells us that demons tremble at the name of Jesus. The devil only have as much power as you give him. If you invite the devil in, he will dwell within you. If you rebuke him, he will flee from you. If you let him; he will come in to kill, steal and destroy everything that is at his possession. There is one thing that I am certain of; when you tell him to go, then he has to go!!!

## Spiritual Food For Thought

**Proverbs 23:7** *states:* [7] *For as he thinketh in his heart, so is he: Eat and drink, saith he to thee; but his heart is not with thee.*

## Self Dialog

The mind is a key with power and it shapes, makes and mold your life. You can let what happened to you in life build you and make you strong in mind, body and soul; or you can let what happened to you break you. Both biological and social psychiatric disorders can cause mood swings, nervous breakdowns, dysfunctional family life, poverty, low self-esteem, anxiety, anger, loneliness, eating disorders and substance abuse.

Unbelievably, these are the many generational curses that are passed down from generation to generation. I declare and decree that these strongholds loose your life and those of your loved ones. I have experienced and seen many things going on in my family. I did not think anything of the lifestyles that I have witnessed growing up as a young girl. I believed that what I had experienced and seen was a normal way of living. My mindset accepted the fact that things happen and it is out of my control. I come to tell you that somethings are out of our control and somethings we can control. The things that we can control we sometimes choose to do nothing about because it feels good and become an adopted lifestyle. There is an army of unclean spirits that we war against daily and they have taken hold of individuals and families as a whole for many decades. The sad part about it is, these demonic spirits have crept in and intruded the inner man with no intentions on departing. While growing up, I did not know that some of the things that I went through was due to some of the rebellious acts from past generations.

These demonic spirits are always looking for a soul that is vulnerable to latch onto like parasites. They take over by leaching and penetrating their filthiness and poison into ones spirit. These demonic spirits latch on to those who bow down, accept or surrender to ill will (sin). Please understand that spirits transfer. If you do not stay in the presence of God through prayer, fasting and reading the word (Bible). They can transfer by touching or being near. This is why we must be careful of who we entertain.

I grew up seeing single family households. I also grew up seeing some good stable family households that will make a great magazine example of good family values. I grew up seeing physical, emotional and mental abuse among spouses, parents and their children. I grew up seeing the spirit of incest in my family. I grew up seeing family members victimized by the spirit of molestation amongst the men and women. I grew up seeing the struggles of living from paycheck to paycheck. I grew up seeing shacking and fornication. I grew up seeing homosexuality and lesbianism in my family. I grew up seeing men cheating on their wives and wives cheating on their husbands. I also grew up seeing a lot of good God fearing marriages. I grew up seeing health issues amongst my family that made them captive to long term medication due to high blood pressure, asthma, bronchitis, diabetes, migraines and thyroids. I grew up seeing some of the same family member going back and forth to jail making it their permanent residence. I grew up seeing women in my family taking care of the men. The women went to work day and night taking care of the household, while the men slept and did nothing to provide for the household. I also grew up seeing some God fearing men taking care of their family and gave it their best at all times. I grew up seeing alcohol and drug abuse amongst my family. I grew up witnessing verbal abuse amongst family. I grew up around all of this as a little girl. The truth of the matter is, even today, some of my family members and some of your family members or even you are still dealing with these same demonic generational curses today.

## Spiritual Food for Thought

*Ephesians 5:3-14 states:* ³ *But fornication, and all uncleanness, or covetousness, let it not be once named among you, as becometh saints;* ⁴ *Neither filthiness, nor foolish talking, nor jesting, which are not convenient: but rather giving of thanks.* ⁵ *For this ye know, that no whoremonger, nor unclean person, nor covetous man, who is an idolater, hath any inheritance in the kingdom of Christ and of God.* ⁶ *Let no man deceive you with vain words: for because of these things cometh the wrath of God upon the children of disobedience.* ⁷ *Be not ye therefore partakers with them.* ⁸ *For ye were sometimes darkness, but now are ye light in the Lord: walk as children of light:* ⁹ *(For the fruit of the Spirit is in all goodness and righteousness and truth;)* ¹⁰ *Proving what is acceptable unto the Lord.* ¹¹ *And have no fellowship with the unfruitful works of darkness, but rather reprove them.* ¹² *For it is a shame even to speak of those things which are done of them in secret.* ¹³ *But all things that reproved are made manifest by the light: for whatever doth make manifest is light.* ¹⁴ *Wherefore he saith, Awake thou that sleepest, and arise from the dead, and Christ shall give thee light.*

The story of my life (Sheaniqua Clarkson- Batty) who is known in this story as Mahogany that you are about to read about will make you sad, it may make you cry, it will make you laugh, it will make you grateful and most of all, it will bring forth repentance, forgiveness and total surrenderance to Gods will and His ways, leading to healing and deliverance. Buckle your seat belt and travel with me on this journey down my life story in which our Lord and Savior Jesus Christ have graced me to live and testify of His goodness.

## The Journey Begins

Mahogany still forming in her mother's womb had a death warrant put out on her life by satan himself. Shari, Mahogany's mother experienced some complications during the third trimester of her pregnancy leaving Dr. Shaw no other choice but to order her to bed rest, due to the possibility of losing her child. Shari imagined how depressed and uncomfortable that will be for her to stay confined to her bed for the remainder of her pregnancy. The thoughts running through Shari's mind knowing that every move that she made could be fatal to Mahogany's survival.

Shari knew that one wrong move from her could end Mahogany's life before it ever began. Shari dreaded what she had to go through the last couple of months of her pregnancy but she also knew that her daughter was worth her having to stay confined to her bed. The will of God was for Mahogany to survive in-spite of all that she had gone through in her mother's womb. Mahogany had a purpose, she just did not know it yet. July 3, 1979 at 7:00 pm James and Shari gave birth to a beautiful baby girl. James smiled from ear to ear happy about the added addition to the family. Shari celebrated with tears of joy that her baby girl made it into this world healthy and strong. Mahogany embraced the love from both of her parents whom happen to be in an unlawful, unordained relationship that was not covered by God. James and Shari considered themselves as common law married. Where in the bible does it say that God covenant common law marriages? Mahogany came into this world born out of wedlock due to the sinful acts of shacking and fornication.

Mahogany entered into the doors of a broken home and a cheating father who loved his sexual desires and money more than life itself, while Shari handed her life to him on a golden platter. Shari gave James her life and he tore into it piece by piece. Shari could have accomplished a lot in her life but she allowed the spirit of manipulation and a need for what she thought was love to capture her, lock her down and hold her in captivity. James was the kind of man that took care of his family, but if he wanted someone or something bad enough he pursued it until it was in his possession. James stubbornness made him feel as if he did not have to listen to anybody, especially Shari. The thermostat in James and Shari's house consistently set on cool. The cold did not come from the air conditioning unit that came with the house. The cold came from the hardness of James heart and the broken promises that he never intended to fulfill. James struggled to show love and appreciation to the woman he called by common law (wife). James did not know how to love outside of working and paying the bills. Working and taking care of his family needs was love, nothing more and nothing less. James gave gifts and held Shari close only on traditional holidays because he felt obligated to celebrate her on Valentines Day, Mother's Day and Christmas. Whatever happened to I fixed dinner today because I love you or I thought about you today? Whatever happened to because we share a special bond I cherish you for who you are? Those things did not exist in the house of James and Shari. James, Shari and now Mahogany lived in a beautiful red framed fenced in house, but what was happening on the inside of that house was dead, with no hope of restoration. All of the brokenness, heartaches and hidden motives in that house made it condemned. If anybody knew what it was like to feel the opposite of real love it was Shari. James smothered himself in his ego knowing that he had Shari right where he wanted her in the palm of his hands. James sniffed weakness about her. Shari thought that if she held on to the good times they shared he would still be near in her heart, but the truth of the matter was, James was far away, with no intentions on returning. Shari thought that if she held on to the charitable memories of how things use to be between them she would keep her sanity. The things Shari encountered with James could have messed her up mentally leading to a chaotic breakdown. James knew that no matter what he did, said or whom he pursued by lust, Shari life twirled within his life. James parented two children prior to him and Shari's relationship. James had two children born by his first love. What happened in James previous relationship had taken a toll on him causing a negative change. A change that led to bad decisions. During James and Shari so called common law marriage he took interest in other women and their unclean spirits attached themselves to James and James released those spirits into the atmosphere of him and Shari's home, increasing the warfare. James fell into a love triangle that brought in unwanted turbulence. Stephanie, James mistress decided that she no longer wanted to carry the title of a mistress. Stephanie wanted something more. The spirit of revenge, lust, discord and greed consumed Stephanie and charged her to go forth bold and unafraid. James and Shari left their back door unlocked at all times just in-case one of them had misplaced their house key. Without thinking about the consequences James told Stephanie about their backdoor secret. Stephanie saw the perfect opportunity to take hold of what she knew and used it to her advantage. Stephanie's obsession with James provoked her to do whatever it took to move Shari out of the way. Shari was a threat to her and it had to be disposed of quickly. Stephanie took it upon herself to make frequently unscheduled appearances while James and Shari were at work. Stephanie parked in the alley, entered into the backdoor and made herself comfortable in their house, utilizing whatever she could to meet her needs and wants. Stephanie washed her clothes, talked on their phone, ate up their food, laid in their bed and watched their television. Stephanie made herself feel right at home as if she was the woman of the house, and when done she exited the backdoor with no guilt or remorse. Shari came home from work and noticed that the food supply was low, washing powder empty, television left on and people calling their house that she did not even recognize. Shari approached James about the matter at hand but he claimed that he did not know what was going on or why it was happening. Shari left the discussion alone and did not question James any further until the bomb went off and made a loud noise. The spirit of revenge, lust, discord and greed consumed Stephanie and charged her for the second time to go forth bold and unafraid. Stephanie parked in the alley and entered in through the backdoor going about her normal routine until she glanced down at the photo album underneath the coffee table. Stephanie set on the couch, grabbed the photo album, opened it up and despised what her eyes beheld. Stephanie saw her lover standing side by side with Shari resembling everlasting love. Stephanie glided aggressively through the photo album until there were no more pages to turn. The horns on top of her head began to show and immediately a fuse blew within her. Stephanie stormed through the house discouraged, angry and intimidated at the thought of James never leaving Shari. Stephanie could not take it anymore. The time had come for Shari to find out the truth about her man. Stephanie paced throughout the house looking for scissors, a knife, a blade or anything sharp that could cause some serious damage. Stephanie's scavenger hunt ended when she found a pair of scissors tucked away in the kitchen drawer. Stephanie stormed out of the kitchen into the living-room operating under the influence of demonic instructions cutting up every picture that she saw of James, Shari and Mahogany. Stephanie found comfort in cutting out every picture of Shari's face. Stephanie wanted revenge on the woman whom she had to share with. Stephanie demolished every portrait leaving the faces of James, a big hole were Shari once was and Mahogany. Stephanie took a marker and wrote across every picture "I am the next Mrs. Hopkins." Stephanie's fury went into overdrive and she began throwing and kicking around every picture in the album leaving the living-room in a complete mess. Stephanie calmed down after the spirit of revenge, lust, discord and greed accomplished their assignment. Stephanie looked around and saw what she had done. The fact that she had made a mess of their house did not bother her because she wanted Shari to know that her and James are lovers and she had been in their house. Stephanie grabbed her stuff and left the house in a complete disaster. Hours later James and Shari pulled up in the driveway at the same time after a long days work. James entertained Shari with humorous conversation about his chaotic workday. Shari embraced the moment of happiness between them hoping that it would last forever. Shari turned the key to unlock the front door, walked in and thought they had been robbed until she saw all of the pictures scattered all over the couch, coffee table and living-room floor with her face cut out of every single one of them. Shari looked at James knowing that she had solid evidence of a woman being in their house, sending a clear message to Shari that she was not James only lover. Shari looked down at the cutouts of her face that violently spoke to her. Shari picked up the phone to dial 911 but before she could dial the number 9, James yanked the phone out of Shari's hands in Stephanie's defense and told her he will handle the situation. The agony and frustration that built up in Shari reached boiling point. It was one thing for James to cheat, but for the mess to come into her house? Oh she was not having it. Shari accepted many things, but she did not play when it came to her house and her child. Time went on as James and Shari worked on repairing their relationship because James swore to never see Stephanie again.

## Self Dialog

I have learned going through similar life situations. If a person have not surrendered to God, the sin will only be contained for a little while and in a matter of time, it will rise again.

James decided to take the day off to invite Stephanie over to the house to make up for lost time. James did not expect Shari home anytime soon because she usually work a full 8-hour shift. Stephanie delighted in James invitation to come spend some quality time with him. Stephanie liked the thought of possibly getting caught seducing another woman's man. Stephanie parked her car boldly in the driveway occupying Shari's parking space. Old lady Kelly from down the street admired her beautifully maintained lawn through her window when she saw James welcoming and exploring Stephanie in seductive ways that made it known that they were more than just friends. Old lady Kelly called Shari on her lunch break and told her all that she had seen going on between James and this strange woman she seen outside on her porch. Confusion hit Shari's mind because of the unexpected news she just heard. Shari clocked out early and told her boss that she had a family emergency. Shari got in her car, burnt out of the parking lot and sped down the highway as if a stalker was chasing her. Shari did not care about going 30 miles over the speed limit and she surely did not care if a cop caught her speeding. Shari focused on all the events that took place over the last couple of month allowing it to trigger something in her nervous system that clouded her mind with unclean thoughts. Deep down inside Shari hoped that it was all just a lie. Shari turned on Shady Lane where she and James resided. Shari pressed on the breaks and pulled over as if she was a cop assigned to a stake out. Shari stood on guard as if she was about to catch America's most wanted criminal. Shari was too scared to go into her own house to catch James in the act of betrayal. Shari waited anxiously for an hour until she witnessed with her own eyes, the unthinkable, the unimaginable and most unbearable thing that she had ever seen. James came out of the house with Stephanie, talking, holding hands, playing around and smiling at one another barely leaving any room for each other to breath. The rage that rose up in Shari made her lose self-control. The only thing that ran across Shari's mind was all of the things that she had done for James during the ten years they had been together and this is the reward that she reaped for being loving and loyal. "How dare he bring the same woman into our home after she made a mess of the house and exposed his dirt!!!" Shari repeatedly reminded herself on how much time she invested into their relationship performing the wifely duties of cooking his meals, cleaning up his mess, washing his clothes and making love to him regardless of how he treated her. Shari hardly asked James for anything. All she wanted from James was a faithful man that loved her. Shari tried to gather her thoughts but for the life of her she could not think straight. The spirit of rage poisoned her mind with foolish conversation without ceasing. James was too indulged in Stephanie to recognize that Shari was parked a couple of houses down scoping out the scene. James walked Stephanie to her car, opened the door and waved goodbye as she disappeared out of his sight. Shari watched his mistress drive off with her man's heart. Shari shifted the gear out of park and put it in drive. Shari had made up in her mind that she was going to run James over without second thoughts. Shari had enough of the mind games and the emotional roller coaster rides. God knew what was going to take place that day because he sent Dorothy Ann, Shari's mother to check on the family. Little did Dorothy Ann know, that when she got there, she was going to be an intervention for something Shari would have regretted. Dorothy Ann saw her daughter's car parked a couple of houses down from where she originally lived looking at James standing outside getting ready to go into the house. Dorothy Ann pulled over and parked behind Shari. Dorothy Ann did not know what was going on, but she knew that something was not right because her daughter was not parked in front of her own house. Shari looked at James with pure hatred from betrayal. Shari slowly took her foot of the breaks and before pushing the gas pedal full force Dorothy Ann blew the horn until Shari eyes made contact with her eyes. Shari saw the devastating look on her mother's face. Dorothy Ann shook her head at Shari in disagreement with what she was about to do to James. "NO, IT'S NOT WORTH IT, LET IT GO!" Dorothy Ann shouted. James turned around to see who was blowing the horn, and it was then, he saw Shari the mother of his child, his roommate and lover of ten years had seen all that had happened with him and Stephanie. James knew that his dirty laundry had been exposed and there was not a lie he could tell that would justify what she had seen. Dorothy Ann watched Shari every move as she parked her car in the drive way. "Shari go in the house and pack some you and Mahogany's things because you are going to stay with me for a little while." Dorothy Ann stated to make sure that Shari's anger would not cause her to take further revenge into her own hands. Dorothy Ann plan was for Shari to find a place of solitude but the truth of the matter was, she could not stop thinking about James. James gave Shari enough time to calm down before calling her. James called and called begging her to come back home promising her that this time things will be different and that he will end things with Stephanie once and for all. Shari sympathetic heart decided to reason with James and go back home after one night of what was suppose to be a week retreat away from home. Shari entered into that house and the spirit of depression and stress overwhelmed her. In a matter of days, James flesh went out of control times two. His lustful desires took over like an incurable disease. Shari found out in the midst of her dying relationship that her and James were expecting their second child. Somewhere in the midst of all the lust, James went out, had relations and got another woman pregnant shortly after Mahogany was born. James also had to confess to Shari that Stephanie was also pregnant with child. During the ten years of being in a relationship with James he had two kids by two other women and Shari still chose to stay. A lot has happened in that fenced in red house. Low self-esteem and self worth became an infestation that took deep root in Shari. James left the house early the next morning carrying on as normal in his right state of mind. When James returned something was different. James was in a trance. James eyes was blood shot red and bigger than usual. James looked confused. James robotic actions was as if he had been programmed by something evil. Shari tried snapping him out of it but her attempt failed. It appeared as if he was under a spell of witchcraft. James looked at Shari and Mahogany as though they were strangers. James acted as if he wanted to strike Shari because she questioned him about what happened to him. Shari knew that James was many things, but physically violent towards her was not one of them. James behavior was as if he was a puppet controlled by his puppet master. Shari thought to herself after ten years of cleaning, cooking, washing clothes, sex, support and children this is what it came down to. The demonic influence of lust and greed controlled him and withdrew him from his good thing. The one thing Shari feared became a reality. Shari found herself alone, with child and relationship condemned.

# Self Dialog

James was not the only person at fault here. A person will only do as much as you let them do. Once they have that mind control over you, you lose the power to control yourself. My mother gave too much of her energy and time to someone who did not have her best interest at heart. My mother decided to take hold of her own life by moving out of and letting go of that which was condemned. My mother packed up our things without her lover of ten years knowing it and when he came home he found himself alone. My mother moved us from Canwell, Texas to Fort Autom, Texas.

Shari frowned at the thought of falling into a familiar pattern she knew all too well. Shari came into realization that what happened to her mother Dorothy Ann has now happened to her. Shari intended on having a successful career, marriage, children and all the happiness one could obtain but instead she fell into the status of a single parent household. The power generational curses have when they have not been acknowledged, rebuked or cast out. There in Fort Autom, Texas in the month of September Sharron was born. In the city of Fort Autom sin was praised and the practices of Sodom and Gomorrah from the bible days repeated itself all over again. The people in this town dressed to impress with their cooler full of iced down liquor and beer after they have whooped, hollered, shouted, sung, preached and slung snot all over the church. The people in this city filled it with wickedness and witchcraft. This was the place Shari, Sharron and Mahogany called home. This is the turning point in Mahogany's life where she came face to face with many unclean spirits. In this city is where deep dark stubborn roots took hold of Mahogany because of the hurt and pain from unwanted turbulence in her life. This is the place where she endured blood, sweat and tears as well as the place that pushed her to purpose.

## Spiritual Food for Thought

**Proverbs 22:5-6** *states:* [5] *Thorns and snares are in the way of the froward: he that doth keep his soul shall be far from them.* [6] *Train up a child in the way he should go: and when he is old, he will not depart from it.*

# CHAPTER TWO

## *The Valley of Family Incest*

Shari enrolled Mahogany in ABC Daycare Center. Shari's occupation in home health care sometimes permitted her to work a couple of hours into the second shift when they were under staffed. As a single parent Shari resulted to the only option she could afford. Shari found favor with the owner of ABC Daycare because of the bond that was made when her and James was together. Margaret the founder and owner of ABC Daycare had a daughter by the name of Valerie that helped her with the affairs of her daycare facility. Shari employer informed her that it was going to be a late night because they were under staffed. Shari called Margaret and informed her that she will be by to pick up Mahogany within a couple of hours due to mandatory overtime. Margaret needed to run some errands and keeping Mahogany for a couple of more hours was not apart of the her agenda. Margaret instructed her daughter Valerie to look over things while she run errands. Mahogany was always the last kid to leave. Mahogany looked around and found herself all alone with no one to play with. Mahogany grabbed some dolls, saucer plates and tea cups and allowed her imagination to run away with her. Mahogany had all the toys to herself not having a care in the world in what was going on around her, until a voice cried out to her saying "Come to the back room." Mahogany put her playful imagination on hold and responded to Valerie's call. Mahogany stood in front of Valerie anticipating what could be so important that she had to pull away from tea time. Valerie grabbed Mahogany by the hand and told her to lay down on her back. Mahogany out of excitement did as she asks thinking it was a new game that they were about to play. Valerie began kissing on Mahogany in ways that babysitter should not kiss on one another. Valerie touched her in unfamiliar ways on the most sacred and delicate parts of her little body. Mahogany without knowing it, had come face to face with a sexual perversion demon called incest and it took hold of the one she called family. In an instant Mahogany *"Walked through the Valley of Incest"* at the age of four years old. After the spirit of incest was satisfied, it released Valerie and went back into hiding. Valerie stopped, looked down at Mahogany, jumped up and made Mahogany cross her fingers and promise that she would never tell anyone what she had done. Crossing fingers was sacred and it was a trust that could never be broken under any circumstance. Mahogany kept her promise because she loved going to school learning and playing with the other children. Margaret and Valerie treated her very well. Valerie had the ideal room that would take anybody far away on a fantasy adventure. Mahogany loved playing dress up in Valerie's over sized clothes and shoes. Mahogany did not care about what happened in the back room. The bribe alone was enough to keep her silent. Mahogany thought she knew something special that nobody else knew. Mahogany locked the secret of incest in her heart and threw away the key. A little time had past and Mahogany grew a couple of years older and inches taller. Summer time had come and Mahogany's grandmother Grandma Casity decided to plan a get away trip with the grandchildren to a relative's house down in Rhondo, Texas. It was their little summer get away in mid June. This was the perfect time to give the parents a week of peace and rest. Grandma Casity kept everyone together because she believed in family growing up with one another instead of being strangers. The grandchildren looked forward to gathering under the same roof by having fun and making the best of summer break. The day had come and every parent prepared their child's luggage for a weeks stay and dropped them off at Grandma Casity's. Grandma Casity was thrilled to see all of her grandchildren together running circles around her laughing and playing tag. Grandma Casity loaded up the trunk and set everyone according to height. The ride to Rhondo, Texas resembled sardines smashed on top of each other in a can. Finally, after a couple of hours of suffering in an overloaded car they arrived in Rhondo, Texas. The town was the true meaning of the phrase "Ghost town." Grandma Casity made a left turn at the light and traveled down a wide-open red dirt road for 2 miles leading to Aunt Rita's house. Grandma Casity pulled in the driveway and instantly Aunt Rita and her two children bust through the screen door screaming at the top of their lungs stumbling over porch furniture trying to get to Grandma Casity's car. Getting out of the car resembled circus clowns getting ready for a circus act. This was the most overwhelming 30 minutes of greetings, hugs and kisses Mahogany had ever experienced. Everyone settled in and Grandma Casity and Aunt Rita made everyone go outside and play so they could catch up on the latest news in each others lives. Mahogany loved playing and walking around on the warm dirt road twirling her toes deep into the ground. Mahogany let down her two pig tails and turned loose in the wide open country. The aroma of down home cooking captured Mahogany's nose as she enjoyed what seem to be a miniature family reunion of the younger generation. There was one thing on their mind and that was fun, fun and more fun. It was the third day of their summer getaway and they played tag, hide-go-seek and hop scotch until the sky grew dark and the street lights came on. This was the sign that everyone had to be in the house. Grandma Casity had a thing that children should not be outside after the street lights come on. The street lights was a sign of bath time, dinner and bedtime. Grandma Casity slept in Aunt Rita's room, Aunt Rita slept on the couch and all of the cousins male and female slept together in one big room. Sharing a room with her cousins felt like one big slumber party. The excitement that filled the atmosphere was too much to go to sleep right away. Grandma Casity searched for sleep she could not find because of the loud conversations down the hall. Grandma Casity screamed to the top of her lungs "BE QUIET AND GO TO SLEEP!!!" The room became quiet and within minutes everyone carried on ignoring Grandma Casity's annoying squeaky voice. Grandma Casity screamed to the top of her lungs for the second time "BE QUIET AND GO TO SLEEP. THIS IS MY LAST TIME TALKING!!!" This time Grandma Casity demand came out in song. Everyone with a show of hands decided to share stories and enjoy each others company. After fighting sleep, eyelids got heavy and sleep took over and won the fight. In the middle of the night Aunt Rita's children began fiddling with Mahogany and everyone that was in the room. Mahogany felt this touch before. She encountered it before at ABC Daycare center some years ago. How did this sexual sin find her again? Who introduced her cousins to this ungodly behavior? Mahogany and her little cousins laid there and let them do whatever they wanted to do to them. "What are you doing?" ask Danielle. Aunt Rita's son Marvin informed Danielle that they was playing a game called boning. The spirit of incest hid behind another name to hide its filth. This demon called incest went on until it was satisfied and when done, it released them and everyone went back to sleep. The sun rose on the next morning and the daily activities went on as usual, playing, laughing and running around in the hot scorching sun. No one seemed to care about the sexual activity that took place and neither did anyone look at each other differently. No one spoke a word of this game called boning, not even Mahogany. The street lights came on, everyone took their baths, ate their dinner in silence and went off to bed. God sent his angels to watch and protect Mahogany because Grandma Casity made Mahogany sleep in the bed with her because the room was too crowded. Mahogany was the youngest out of the group, so therefore, she had to sleep in the other room with Grandma Casity. Mahogany did not understand why she did not choose someone else to sleep in the bed with her. Mahogany got upset with Grandma Casity because she wanted to take part in this abominable sin called "Incest." The spirit of sexual immorality was waiting for the perfect opportunity for Mahogany to recognize that the desire was there and give it permission to bloom.

# Spiritual Food for Thought

*Leviticus 18:1-20* states: [1] *And the Lord spake unto Moses, saying,* [2] *Speak unto the children of Israel, and say unto them, I am the Lord your God.* [3] *After the doings of the land of Egypt, wherein ye dwelt, shall ye not do: and after the doings of the land of Canaan, whither I bring you, shall ye not do: neither shall ye walk in their ordinances.* [4] *Ye shall do my judgments, and keep mine ordinances, to walk therein: I am the Lord your God.* [5] *Ye shall therefore keep my statutes, and my judgments: which if a man do, he shall live in them: I am the Lord.* [6] *None of you shall approach to any that is near of kin to him, to uncover their nakedness: I am the Lord.* [7] *The nakedness of thy father, or the nakedness of thy mother, shalt thou not uncover: she is thy mother; thou shalt not uncover her nakedness.* [8] *The nakedness of thy father's wife shalt thou not uncover: it is thy father's nakedness.* [9] *The nakedness of thy sister, the daughter of thy father, or daughter of thy mother, whether she be born at home, or born abroad, even their nakedness thou shalt not uncover.* [10] *The nakedness of thy son's daughter, or of thy daughter's daughter, even their nakedness thou shalt not uncover: for theirs is thine own nakedness.* [11] *The nakedness of thy father's wife's daughter, begotten of thy father, she is thy sister, thou shalt not uncover her nakedness.* [12] *Thou shalt not uncover the nakedness of thy father's sister: she is thy father's near kinswoman.* [13] *Thou shalt not uncover the nakedness of thy mother's sister: for she is thy mother's near kinswoman.* [14] *Thou shalt not uncover the nakedness of thy father's brother, thou shalt not approach to his wife: she is thine aunt.* [15] *Thou shalt not uncover the nakedness of thy daughter in law: she is thy son's wife; thou shalt not uncover her nakedness.* [16] *Thou shalt not uncover the nakedness of thy brother's wife: it is thy brother's nakedness.* [17] *Thou shalt not uncover the nakedness of a woman and her daughter, neither shalt thou take her son's daughter, or her daughter's daughter, to uncover her nakedness; for they are her near kinswomen: it is wickedness. [18] Neither shalt thou take a wife to her sister, to vex her, to uncover her nakedness, beside the other in her life time. [19] Also thou shalt not approach unto a woman to uncover her nakedness, as long as she is put apart for her uncleanness. [20] Moreover thou shalt not lie carnally with thy neighbour's wife, to defile thyself with her.*

## Self Dialog

The Lord had given Moses instructions to the people on what to do and what not to do long before my generation. Therefore, this tells me that the generation I was born into was subject to obey the instructions of the Lord that were written. I often wondered. Where was the ball dropped? Where and when did the practice of incest start in my family? I often wondered. Did incest come from loneliness so someone found an interest in a family member? Why was incest so strong amongst my generation? How did the spirit of Sodom and Gomorrah poison the hearts of my family? How did the spirit of Lott's daughters creep into my family tree? Why is it that the seasoned ones in the family did not discern it and cast those unclean spirits out? Was the sin so deep and hidden into the heart that no one took the time to notice that there was a spiritual defect going on? Some of my family and their friends gathered together many weekends anointing each other, praying, rebuking and fell out in the spirit. How is that other demons were discerned and cast out, but the sin of lust and incest stayed? Could it be that no one wanted to admit that there was a problem? Could it be that no one wanted to expose these sinful acts out of guilt and embarrassment? Time went on and all of my relatives departed ways into different parts of the United States making us strangers to one another. I have not seen a lot of my relatives in decades. Separation took place and allowed healing and deliverance to enter the mind, heart and spirit. I heard about the good things that had taken place in the lives of those that participated in family incest. The ones that took part in this sexual sin are now saved, married, raising their children, owning businesses and operating in ministry. Somewhere and somehow those demonic spirits was recognized and the choice to repent and purge took place. The portion of my family that did this, did not whither and die in this sin called incest. I believe every participant got on their face before the Lord and ask him for forgiveness to wash away unwanted filth, even I repented because I got mad at my grandmother because I wanted to take part in this ungodly act. God spared our lives and forgave us. God restored what came to destroy character, dignity, and purity. I thank God for the great washing that took place in my family. I thank God that he purged and he circumcised that which was defiled. The Lord dissected what was poisonous and restored life. I thank God that my family turned from their wicked ways. I thank God for life once again; for we as a family went through *"The Valley of the Incest"*

# CHAPTER THREE

## *The Valley of Molestation #1*

Mahogany enjoying her youth participated in multiple activities to occupy her time. Mahogany extra curricular activities consist of basketball, church drill team and girl scouts. Mahogany's happiness showed from the inside out until she took a crash course of nature 101. Mahogany coming into her own took on the transition of woman hood at the age of 11 years old. Mahogany woke up with unbearable intense pain at 2:00 in the morning. Mahogany bald up in her bed like she was taken shelter because of a bad storm. The pain in Mahogany's abdomen and womb felt like a rope tied in many knots. Mahogany called for her mother as she ran into the closet size bathroom. Shari panicked, jumped up and ran in after her daughter's frantic voice. Mahogany looked up at her mother with such fright on her face because the seat of her pajama pants was covered in blood. Mahogany had an encounter with nature for the first time. The nurturing side of Shari coached Mahogany on how to take care of herself during that time of the month. Shari gave Mahogany aspirin to help ease the pain and bring comfort. Shari gently brushed her fingers through Mahogany's hair, kissed her forehead and sent her to bed. The following day Mahogany's pain from nature was still too much to bare. Shari have never left Mahogany at home by herself. Shari believed in parental supervision at all times. Shari called Grandma Casity her ex mother-in-law by common law marriage. Shari despised having to call Grandma Casity for a favor but who else could she call in such short notice whom she trusted with her daughters well being. Shari swallowed her pride and asked if Mahogany could stay with her until she got off of work due to her encounter with nature. Mahogany listened to her mother reveal all of her personal business to Grandma Casity. Mahogany did not want anyone knowing what she was going through, it was too embarrassing. Grandma Casity understood being that she have traveled down that road as a mother with her own daughters. Grandma Casity sympathized with Shari and agreed to keep Mahogany. Grandma Casity's heart went out to anyone in need. Shari pulled in the drive way about 7:00 am blowing the horn while grabbing Mahogany's bag out of the back seat making Grandma Casity aware of their arrival. Shari did not get out of the car because she was pressed for time. Besides, Grandma Casity will get her pay docked for talking too much. Mahogany walked in and found out that her cousin Jack had been staying with Grandma Casity. Mahogany always thought that there was something strange about Jack. The way he looked at people was disturbing. Mahogany redirected her focus to Grandpa Jimmy. Mahogany ran around the house eagerly searching for him but he had already left for work. Grandpa Jimmy plumbing skills gave him the reputation of being the greatest plumber of all time. He could fix anything with his eyes closed. The employees at Leon Ducket Plumbing Service compared him to life support; because without him it could not survive. Mahogany shrugged her shoulders at the fact of having to stay with Grandma Casity and Jack. Mahogany arrived just in time for breakfast. Grandma Casity cooked her daily morning special of rice, dear sausage and a cup of sugared down kool-aid to wash it down. Mahogany have never known her grandmother to cook anything else different at breakfast time. Mahogany set at the wooden round table, said her grace and took a spoon full of sugared down rice and went in for the dear sausage. Mahogany stuffed herself until she did not have anymore room to store food. Mahogany excused herself from the table, went into the living-room and laid down on the pastel colored couch. The medicine Shari gave her before going to Grandma Casity's had set in bringing relief to Mahogany's pain. Mahogany grabbed Grandma Casity's hand made quilt that was folded up so nicely on the couch, covered up and allowed sleep to consume her. Mahogany's nap was short lived. Grandma Casity woke Mahogany up out of her sleep with the gentle touch of her index finger. Mahogany looked up and saw that Grandma Casity was dressed to leave. Grandma Casity had on her hand made dress, brown coffee stockings, nursing shoes and a salt and pepper colored wig that set perfectly on her head. Grandma Casity social security check had come in the mail so she needed to go deposit her money and pay a couple of bills. "I'll be back Mahogany. Your cousin Jack will watch after you until I get back." Jack nodded his head at Grandma Casity accepting the responsibility given to him. Mahogany looked at Jack and saw the look in his eyes and the smirk on his face. The look he gave was nothing like she had ever seen before. "Can I go with you Grandma Casity...?" "No Mahogany, I will only be gone for a little while and I don't want you to mess up your clothes." "Please......" Mahogany begged. "I don't want to stay. I need the fresh air." Grandma Casity looked at Mahogany with sharp piercing eyes. "No Mahogany, now hush!" "Be a good girl and watch television." "I'll be back before you know it; besides your cousin Jack will watch you." Jack watching her raised a warning flag. From the look of things Jack had already been watching and not in a way a babysitter watches a child. Grandma Casity grabbed her purse and left out the house humming an unknown tune that only she enjoyed. Mahogany's eyes followed Grandma Casity from the living-room window until she got in her car. Something in Mahogany wanted to disobey Grandma Casity, run after her and jump in the car. Mahogany did not want a whipping because she knew how her grandparents felt about a disobedient child. Mahogany knew that her grandparents did not believe in sparing the rod or compromising. When they said something the first time, that was the final answer without any negotiation. Grandma Casity and Grandpa Jimmy had a way of getting one's attention when it came to discipline. Mahogany never experienced the whippings from her grandparents, but she sure felt the others pain. Mahogany set still and decided not to run after her. Grandma Casity pulled out of the drive way and Jack eyes followed her out of the window until the car was no longer visible in his sight. Mahogany did not even acknowledge that Jack was in the same room with her. Mahogany kept her eyes glued to the cartoon that took her interest. For some reason Jack spirit was not settled and his behavior became very abnormal. Jack got up from the couch and began pacing back and forth from the living-room to the kitchen. After pacing back and forth a couple of times Jack set on the couch across from Mahogany and began staring at her like a kid that want to catch the attention of his parents when they want a snack. "What are you watching Mahogany?" Mahogany ignored Jack because she knew that Jack was asking a question that he already knew the answer to. "I want to show you how your dad and your mom did it?" Mahogany frowned up her face. "Did what?" Jack did not answer her, instead he acted. Jack grabbed Mahogany, held his hand over her mouth, took her to the back room, tide her down with his body and had his way with her. The one she called family betrayed, hurt and took her body and defiled it. In an instant Mahogany *"Walked through the Valley of Molestation."* When that demon called molestation was satisfied, it made Mahogany promise to never tell what he had done. Mahogany agreed and that demon released Jack and went back into hiding.

## Self Dialog

When a person like dwelling in sin their heart becomes harden to truth. Something had been going on with my cousin prior to the time this incident took place. Jack had been going through something mentally and emotionally on the inside for a long time. Whatever was going on with Jack he chose to let it linger instead of confronting it by seeking help. Jack allowed whatever he was dealing with become an infestation in his heart, mind and soul which led to ungodly sexual acts of molestation. Throughout Jacks life he had been to prison for messing with under age girls. I did not know then, but I know now. It was not Jack that molested me. It was that demon that had a stronghold over him that molested me.


Grandma Casity pulled up in the driveway a couple of hours later. Jack looked at Mahogany and gave her that you better not try anything silly look. Grandma Casity came in the house, smiling and humming as she always do with sacks full of groceries and a bag full of goodies for her and Sharron to snack on. Grandma Casity asked Mahogany if she was feeling any better but Mahogany lied, knowing that she felt the opposite of better. What Mahogany really wanted to do was bust out in tears and tell her what Jack had done. Mahogany did not say a word. Instead she held her pain deep within, only to be left scorned. The encounters of incest and molestation had taken a toll on her. After Grandma Casity set the groceries on the table she came back into the living-room, looked down at Mahogany and saw that she had on the change of clothes that her mother prepared for her as a backup. Grandma Casity chuckled. "Didn't I tell you that you was going to mess up your clothes?" Mahogany looked at her, smiled and shook her head. "Yes ma'am you sure did." Grandma Casity went into the kitchen and began preparing her everyday lunch special red beans and cornbread. Mahogany took Grandma Casity presence in the house as a sign of protection from the boogie man. Jack relieved at the fact that Mahogany complied with his instructions. Jack struck up a conversation with Grandma Casity and began helping her pick out the bad beans from the good beans. Jack put on the identity of a comedian and laughter filled the kitchen. The hurt in Mahogany's eyes when Grandma Casity did not notice that something was wrong. Mahogany's sister Sharron made it in from school happy and full of life. Time went by, evening approached and Shari's workday came to an end. Jack wanted to make sure that there was no room for tattle tales. Shari pulled in the driveway, blew the horn, got out of the car and entered the house. When Shari saw Jack she paused at the fact of seeing Jack in the house. Shari had a look on her face that if looks could kill, Jack would be dead. Jack smiled and greeted Shari with no conviction. "Hello Jack." "Oh, just in-case you are wondering what I am doing here, I will be staying with Grandma Casity's for a while until I get back on my feet." Shari thinking to herself if she had known she would have called in and took care of Mahogany herself. Sharron and Mahogany gathered their things, said their goodbye's and got in the car. Shari noticed that Mahogany was not herself. "Why are you so quiet Mahogany?" "Your not running off at the mouth about your day." Shari discerned Mahogany's nonchalant attitude. "Turn around Mahogany and look at me." Mahogany ignored her mother's instructions and kept looking out of the side window hoping that she would leave it alone. Shari asked Mahogany for the second time. "Turn around and look at me." Once again Mahogany ignored her mother's wishes. The tone in Shari's voice changed. "I'm not going to tell you again Mahogany, turn around and look at me!" Mahogany turned around and looked at her mother and surrendered to the fact that she could no longer fight back the tears that she tried to suppress. Mahogany ashamed of what happened to her, put her head in the palm of her hands and the tears seeped through the cracks of her fingers like a bad leak in a faucet pipe. Shari terrified of what could possibly be bothering her child. Sharron started crying because Mahogany was crying. Shari calmed Mahogany down with her soft voice, told her to take a deep breath and tell her everything that had happened. Shari reassured Mahogany that nothing would happen to her. Mahogany with her head held down slowly looked up at her mother. "Yes it will. He said it would." Shari reassured Mahogany that she would not get in trouble for telling her what's on her mind. Mahogany felt a little comfortable and at ease and proceeded in telling her mother in detail what happened to her. Mahogany had never seen her mother so blanked out a day in her life. Shari was the kind of woman that always wore a smile no matter the situation. On that particular day and at that particular time, that smile was no more. Mahogany had never seen her mother so outraged. In the midst of all that, the thought that came to Shari's mind was to pray. Mahogany was a bit confused at her mother's reaction to the situation. "How can she pray at a time like this?" Mahogany thought to herself. What Mahogany wanted was for her mother to go and beat the mess out of him. Shari finished praying and called James. Tears fell from Shari's eyes while trying to tell James that their daughter had been violated by family. James hung up the phone in the middle of Shari's conversation and before she knew it, James was parked in front of her house. James must have been going 100mph down the highway to get to Shari's house as fast as he did. Mahogany's father forced her to tell him everything that had happened all over again. James stormed out of the house, got in his car and went to his mother's house to confront Jack. James rushed in his mother's house without saying a word to anyone. James searched the house asking for Jack. Grandma Casity was a bit confused and demanded that he calm down and tell her what was going on with him. James looked at his mother, kept silent and walked past her, picked up the phone and called Shari. James informed Shari that Jack was not there but he was going to stay there until he came back. Hours had past and the beauty of the sun began to set. James made it known that he did not care if he had to be there all night and miss work. James was determined to stay put and get answers. Jack saw James car parked in the driveway. Jack did not know whether to turn around or be bold. Jack took a chance and went into the house. James did not asks Jack any questions, he allowed his fist to do the talking. It was after James physical response to Jack's behavior he was able to asks questions. "Why did you do it?" James gave Jack no time to respond. James walked away and assured him that his sick behavior will have consequences. James left his mother's house, huffing and puffing, mad and breathing heavy. James arrived back at Shari's house and shortly after the telephone rung. Shari answered and on the other end was Grandma Casity with a snappy attitude demanding to speak with James. James took the phone and his mother began fussing at him on Jack's behalf.

"You know that Jack would never do such a thing to Mahogany!" James took a deep breath and cut her off before she could say another word. "Mom, I love you, but I am not going to stand here and listen to your foolishness." "I won't stand here and let you talk about my daughter and defend a child molester." James hung up the phone and Grandma Casity was greeted by a dial tone. James instructed Shari to keep Mahogany from visiting her grandmother until Jack was gone for good. James and Shari called the police and filed a police report. The investigating police took every description from head to toe. They documented the color of his hair, skin, eyes and every marking on his body. The Fort Autom police department left nothing unturned. Jack thought that since he denied it that he was going to get away with it. Immediately after gathering the information needed, the investigating officers went to Grandma Casity's house and arrested Jack. Jack stayed in the Fort Autom county jail until his court date. Mahogany was satisfied, but not satisfied enough. While waiting for the court date Shari and Mahogany went through hell with her father's side of the family. They told Shari that all this was because her daughter wanted attention and there was no way that Jack was capable of committing such a crime. Mahogany did not understand why the one's she called family threw stones at her for a relative that mishandled and abused her sexually. Mahogany had a Jesus and Barabbas encounter. Jesus own people rather release the criminal into society and crucify an innocent man. They disowned her and left her and Shari alone traveling down a long lonely road to recovery. Mahogany went into hiding until everything blew over. Time had past and Mahogany went back to her normal self until it was time to come face to face with Jack in court. The judge decided to let her testify on the stand without Jack being present in the room since she was a minor. "Why does this court proceeding have to be so long?" Mahogany said to herself. Mahogany waited with great anticipation of the verdict from Judge Markee. Judge Markee finally reached his verdict after a long deliberation and to Mahogany's surprise the court ruled in Jack's favor because they said it was not enough evidence. Mahogany's parents furious at the judges decision blamed themselves because they did not take Mahogany to the doctor to get examined as proof. Mahogany knew that her parents were big on not letting family business get out into the community. Mahogany spirit broke with no hope of repair. Mahogany's heart could not take it anymore. Mahogany lashed out in anger making a bold statement. "I guess I would have to be almost dead in order for justice to be done." The man that hurt her and took her innocents was free and back in society.

# CHAPTER FOUR

## *The Valley of Hiding in Isolation*

The spirit of isolation, fear and depression nested in Mahogany's fainting soul. These unclean spirits began eating away at her like termites feasting on wood. Mahogany's spirit man began to decay from all of the criticism, hurt and loneliness that she felt. Mahogany lived under a dark cloud with no chance of sun peaking through it. It hunted her. Mahogany could not take anymore of the lies, criticisms, deceit and violations that kept piercing her in the back time after time again. Mahogany decided that she no longer wanted to stand face to face with her past or present. The only thing Mahogany wanted to do was shut down, run and tuck herself away in isolation. Mahogany developed paranoia believing that someone was watching her, only to come after her and hurt her. Mahogany's appetite for food decreased and her attitude for revenge increased. Life took a toll on Mahogany. The devil had her right where he wanted her. Mahogany retaliated against anyone who acted as if they wanted to harm her. Mahogany even took her frustrations out on her peers at school. Mahogany's classmate Jamaal picked on her and teased her because he liked her. Mahogany thought to herself "If he liked me, he have a funny way of showing it." Mahogany did not know much about the signs of flirting, but she knew that the way Jamaal was showing it, it felt like the hurt she experienced in her past. Jamaal teased and bullied Mahogany for the last time. Mahogany took vengeance into her own hands and retaliated against him. Mahogany punched Jamaal, picked him up, threw him over the cafeteria table onto the hard floor, where he hit his head knocking him unconscious. The cafeteria that once filled with laughter and premature conversations became silent for just a moment. The silence broke with the cries of confused students and teachers running to Jamaal's rescue dialing 911 for emergency assistance. Mahogany had given the spirit of anger permission to enter and use her. Mahogany's anger towards Jamaal took her back to that place she did not want to revisit. Mahogany's bad decision reaped suspension from school for a few days. Mahogany became isolated from family and now her friends. Mahogany had so much free time on her hands in isolation she allowed her mind to think about all of the hurt, pain, wound and scars she had encountered throughout her lifetime. Mahogany had not forgiven her family for the countless sexual acts towards her, so that was the perfect opportunity for her to take her frustrations out on Jamaal. Mahogany felt deep hurt and wanted someone else to feel her pain. Mahogany retaliated and after the damage was done, it scared her. Mahogany allowed the enemy to work on her mind by installing bitterness and un-forgiveness.

## *Self Dialog*

I went into a state of isolation because I did not want to be hurt and disappointed by people. I had suffered greatly during the 11 years of my life. I was tired of being the victim of others unclean monsters. I was tired of people throwing me in the pit and accusing me of jumping in on my own free will. I was tired of feeling unaccepted and unloved. I was tired of people treating and looking at me like I was less than nothing. I grew tired of the pain and tears. I took bricks (circumstances in life) and built a wall because I was tired. I felt safe behind the wall, so I thought. The trick of the enemy cut me off from society, left me in isolation and did not stop talking until he wore me down into a suicidal state (death). Everybody around me irritated me whether they did something or not. *"I Walked through the Valley of the Isolation."*

## Spiritual Food for Thought

*Psalms 23 states: [1] The Lord is my shepherd; shall not want. He maketh me to lie down in green pastures: he leadeth me beside the still waters. He restoreth my soul: he leadeth me in the paths of righteousness for his name's sake. Yea, though I walk through the valley of the shadow of death, I will fear no evil: for thou art with me; thy rod and thy staff they comfort me. Thou preparest a table before me in the presence of mine enemies: thou anointest my head with oil; my cup runneth over. Surely goodness and mercy shall follow me all the days of my life: and I will dwell in the house of the Lord for ever. Amen.*

## Self Dialog

My mother constantly took my sister and I to church. The scripture that my mother taught me repeated itself in my mind time after time again. There is a saying that says "Whatever you put in your head is what's going to show on the outside." After quoting Psalms 23 daily. I started believing that God was my comforter and my protector even though *"I Walked through the Valley of Isolation."* God had a way of escape planned out for me. I just needed to believe and trust him with my life. I had to prophesy to my spirit at a young age. I had to encourage and uplift myself at a young age. This is how I overcame the obstacles before me. I became victorious in the valley of dry bones. Those things which I thought was dead came alive. I went out into society again and it felt good. I gained courage to go around the other side of my family and it felt good. I had to inherit the spirit or Ezekiel prophesying to things that were dead around me. That is what you must do in order to defeat the devil. You have to make him out of a liar in-spite of what it looks like past or present. You have to have the mindset that you will not shy away behind the wall. You have to encourage yourself that no matter what it look or feel like, I will not dwell in self-pity in spite of the turmoil going on around me. I will move forward and exalt into where God wants me to be spiritually, mentally and emotionally. I will not allow what happened to me keep me from what God has in store for me. At a young age I embraced the spirit of Ezekiel. I made up in my mind that I was going to speak to everything that was going on around me. I had made up in my mind that I wanted these old bones to live. Don't let your past mountains, your past hurtles, your past tornado, hurricanes, hell storms and strong winds keep you from the purpose that God has destined for you. If I spoke to my storm, surely you can speak to yours. It does not matter if it was 30, 20, 10, 5 years ago, 6 months ago or even yesterday. God got you and he just want you to trust and have faith in him. In order for God to move in your life you have to move out of his way, let him work and stand in faith knowing that it is already done in Jesus Name.

## Self Dialog

Let's touch and agree in prayer. I speak to that spirit that have you hiding behind the walls of the dark place (death). Spirit of isolation I rebuke, bind and sever your head under the power of the Holy Ghost! I command you to loose your grip off of their life, for you no longer have possession over their mind, heart and spirit! I send you spirit of isolation back to the dry places that you came from and I command you to whither and die in the mighty name of Jesus! I declare and decree that you will arise sons and daughter's of God and come forth with your war clothes on ready to fulfill purpose in the mighty name of Jesus! It is so. You have been renewed, restored and re-established in Jesus Mighty Name! Amen.

# CHAPTER FIVE

## *The Valley of Molestation # 2*

Shari, Sharron and Mahogany shared a one bedroom, one bath home that set on a little hill close to a deep dirty creek filled with all kinds of trash and creepy crawling bugs. The house was so in tune with the creek, it appeared as if it could have falling in at anytime. The house came with an unwanted amenity. The landlord failed to reveal to Shari that there was a serious snake infestation because of the creek and they seem to find ways to get into the house. These were no ordinary snakes. These snakes were clever. They did not enter into any part of the house. They always let themselves in through the kitchen, as if they knew that is where the snacks were stored. Sharron and Mahogany wanted a midnight snack before going to bed. Mahogany took the lead and Sharron trailed behind her because she was afraid of the dark. Mahogany stepped into the entryway of the kitchen, turned on the light and discovered a lump in the rug that had not been there before. Mahogany thought the lump appeared because of much needed repairs. Mahogany lifted the rug and found a snake caught underneath it looking for a way out. Fright came over Sharron and Mahogany's face as they looked at their unexpected guest. Mahogany threw the rug down with hopes of trapping the snake back under it, but the snake crawled away quickly scared for it's life. Sharron and Mahogany did not know that the snake was scared of them just as much as they were scared of the snake. Inspite of the snake infestation Shari,

Sharron and Mahogany did not complain because they had a place to call their own. Besides, there were families that lived in worse conditions. The screams from the depths of their belly woke Shari up out of her sweet and peaceful sleep. Shari went into the kitchen, grabbed the bag of snake poisoning and sprinkled it around the base of the kitchen floor. Shari, Sharron and Mahogany went on about their life enjoying every bit of mother and daughter time together. There was no tears of sorrow; but there was tears of joy. There was no trace of drama; but there was peace. There was no trace of turbulence; but there was comfort. Peace, joy and comfort was rattled and disturbed on a Saturday night about 8:00 pm when Sharron and Mahogany heard a knock at the door. Sharron and Mahogany ran to the window eager to find out who could be knocking on their door in the dark hours of the night. Sharron and Mahogany pulled back the curtains and to their surprise appeared a 6 foot tall man that had a friendly look about him. Shari quickly prepped herself in the mirror, went to the door with a boomerang smile on her face, greeted him and ushered him in with the signal of her hand. "Hi, my name is Damian." Damian greeted Sharron and Mahogany with a big smile and a hug to seal his introduction. "What are you doing here Mr. Damian?" Mahogany asks probing in her mother's business. "I come to pay you all a visit." He replied. Sharron and Mahogany looked at each other with excitement because they were not use to having company. The experience Shari had with James made her give up the company of a man. Damian presented himself well and appeared to have the good sense God gave him. Things became very serious with Damian and Shari in a short period of time. Damian thought it was time for his family to find out how serious he was about the woman in his life. Damian made plans for Shari, Sharron and Mahogany to meet his family. Damian's family hosted a welcome to the family gathering that resembled football fans having a tailgate party in the parking lot of a football stadium. Sharron and Mahogany had the luxury of being in the company of peers their age instead of keeping each other company. Damian's family knew how to entertain their guest and each other. The lay out was remarkable and it was like nothing

Sharron and Mahogany had ever seen before. The tables was covered with food buffet style in and without the house. Dozens of people surrounded the domino table waiting for the opportunity to play, while Damian and his relatives played basketball on dirt and rocks, slam dunking on a hand made basketball goal that was hammered to the light post. The loud yelling and talking noise during the basketball game was a lot like the action you saw on the Jerry Springer Show. Damian's family treated Shari, Sharron and Mahogany like family. Damian and Shari decided that they were soul-mates and took their relationship to another level. Dating turned into an engagement within five months of knowing one another. Sharron and Mahogany felt mixed emotions about their mother getting married so quickly. Sharron and Mahogany did not know what to expect when it came to who will get the most love and attention. What was meant to be a household for three will soon become a household of four. The thought of their mother getting married did not set well with them at all. A matter of fact it looked distorted.

## Self Dialog

There is such thing as love at first sight. Yes, people do get married after a couple of months of knowing each other and it's a God ordained marriage. In this case Damian and my mother's engagement was not of God. Neither of them consulted God first before getting engaged or married. In result to self will and being anxious, it cost my mother more than she bargained for. Words of wisdom to those who desire to marry. During the courting/dating stages make sure that you are in tune with God to hear so you won't miss. If he or she is talking marriage make sure that you consult God first and make sure he or she is the one sent to walk by your side for life, because if not, destruction will surely follow.

## Spiritual Food for Thought

**Philippians 4:6-7** *states:* [6] *Be careful for nothing; but in every thing by prayer and supplication with thanksgiving*

*let your requests be made known unto God. [7] And the*
*peace of God, which passeth all understanding, shall*
*keep your hearts and minds through Christ Jesus.*

The wedding took two weeks of preparation. The wedding plans was small and simple. James sister took the liberty of hosting Damian and Shari's wedding at her house. Margaret and Shari had become best friends and they would do anything for each other in-spite of the failed relationship between her and James. Shari became Mrs. Phelps. A short time had past and the true identity of Damian showed up with his horns on fire. Damian left the house and came back intoxicated from consuming too much alcohol. Damian shouted, kicked and banged on the door like a mad man disrupting the peace of nearby neighbors. Shari put on her robe, walked into the living-room, cut on the light, peeked through the window and saw Damian standing there acting like a juvenile child. "OPEN THE DOOR!" Damian demanded. Shari was a bit confused in the force behind his voice. "Damian there is no way that you are getting into this house drunk and out of control." Mahogany could see the fear rising up in her mother's eye's. Shari swallowed and took a deep breath because she did not want Sharron and Mahogany to see her panic. Damian stubbornness did not want to process the fact that he was not going to get into the house acting like a menace to society. The demonic spirit of alcoholism and anger persuaded him that he was going to get into the house whether voluntarily or involuntarily. Damian put his weight against the door and pushed up against it to force an entry. It was then, Shari calmness went out of the window. Shari had a little surprise of her own. Shari instructed Mahogany to help her move the couch in front of the door as a bearer. Sharron began screaming and hollering from the fright that over shadowed her. Shoot, they all experienced fright from dealing with a psycho. Shari made it know to Damian that if he did not leave, she was going to have him arrested. It was evident that jail was the last place Damian wanted to go because he jetted out of there like a man having a serious case of diarrhea. Shari stayed up all night pacing backwards and forwards throughout the house on guard for her and her daughters safety. Two days had passed when Damian decided to come back home. Damian explained why Shari had not seen him in a couple of days. Damian told Shari that he could not show his face because of the shameful things that he had done to her, the children and himself. Damian apologies was drawn out, pathetic and manipulative. Damian squeezed tears from his eyes expressing himself through hand gestures to accompany his rehearsed speech. Damian explained to Shari how marriage was new to him and it was all overwhelming. Damian sealed his speech by explaining to Shari that two days to himself allowed him to clear his head. Damian could have gotten an academy award for best actor. He was that good in dramatic role playing. Shari took him back just in-case he was really nervous about marriage. Shari comforted him and assured him that whatever he was going through, they were going to get through it together. Mahogany knew that was an excuse to take him back because she did not want to be alone. After all, Damian was her husband and she honored the vows "For better or for worse." Damian and Shari decided that it was time for a bigger space and decided to go house hunting. After two weeks of searching they found and leased a white and blue framed house that set on the corner of Smith and Regal Street. The new house consist of two bedrooms, one bath and without snake infestation. Even though Mahogany and Sharron shared the same room, they both loved the fact of no longer having to share a room with their mother and new step-dad. However, the floor plan did not go in Sharron and Mahogany's favor. When guest came to visit they had a clear view of their bedroom exposing everything they had from decorations, to the color on the wall and the type of bed that they slept in. The only room in the house that had doors was the bathroom and the master bedroom. After a week of unpacking and cleaning Damian disappeared and so did Shari household belongings. Damian theft started off small and got bigger each time he went on a stealing spree. Shari took Sharron and Mahogany out for a day of fun to take her mind off of her current situation to focus on what really mattered most. After a long day of fun Shari,

Sharron and Mahogany came home and discovered that their VCR and expensive unused silverware sets was missing. Damian came home later that evening and Shari questioned him about the missing items that vanished from the house. Damian scoffed at Shari's probing questions about the missing items that mysteriously disappeared. Shari made it known to Damian that she had those items for years and not once have they came up missing. "I guess they grew feet and ran away." Shari stated in a sarcastic tone. Shari took a good look at her husband and realized that the man she married was a drug addict and alcoholic. Damian did not bother giving Shari any kind of explanation instead he stormed out of the house and slammed the screen door behind him. Shari took a deep breath and ask Mahogany to accompany her in a game of Monopoly. They were well into the game and it was Mahogany's turn to role the dice. Mahogany cupped the dice in the palm of her hands, shook them real good and rolled them out on the game board rolling a seven. "I passed go. I want to collect my two hundred dollars!!!" In the midst of all the excitement an old friend of Shari knocked on the screen door asking if she had a minute to spare. Shari excused herself from the living-room table, walked outside and escorted him to the other side of the porch to speak in private. Mahogany knew that whatever it was had to be important that they had to discuss whatever it was at the other end of the porch. Mahogany could not take not knowing what all of the secret talk was about. Mahogany got up from the table and set in the recliner by the screen door listening to their every word. "Shari be very careful and most of all watchful. The man you married tried to sell me an item that was stolen out of your house." "Out of respect for you and our friendship, I declined it due to the guilt that would have come over me, if I had accepted it." Shari thanked him, excused herself from the conversation, grabbed a permanent marker and wrote her name on everything that she thought Damian could carry out of the house and sell big and small. Damian came home from his none productive day and saw what Shari had done. The look on his face when he found out that he could no longer take and sell Shari and the girls belongings. Damian did whatever he had to do in order to relieve him of that addict craving. Damian started stealing money out of Shari's purse while she was asleep. The demonic spirit of substance abuse controlled him and had his mind so far gone that he did not care if his family did not have a roof over their head, water to drink or lights to see. Many times Shari faced eviction because she fell behind on paying the rent. Damian spent every dime leaving Shari no choice but to borrow money from family and friends. Shari had enough and decided that something had to give because he was not going to keep taking the hard earned money that she worked for so he can get high. Shari came up with another plan and hid her purse beside Mahogany's bed against the wall. Christmas had come and the spirit of joy filled the air. It was two days before Christmas and while everyone was sound asleep Damian stole all of Sharron and Mahogany's Christmas presents. For the first time Sharron and Mahogany had an encounter with the Grinch that stole Christmas. The Grinch came from television to reality. Shari called the police and waited for their arrival. The investigating cops took down a good description of Damian and everything that was stolen. Shari turned her back away from Sharron and Mahogany and whispered to the police. "I can replace everything else. I just need my children Nintendo and the four hundred dollar keyboard that my mother bought Mahogany." Somehow, with the help of cops they retrieved the keyboard from the person that purchased it from Damian. Sharron and Mahogany's heart crushed with so much hurt and disappointment knowing that Christmas would never be the same. A week later Damian had the nerve to show up quoting the same rehearsed speech as before. "I am sorry. I won't do it again. I don't know what came over me." Once again, the love and sympathy Shari had for him accepted his apology and welcomed him back with open arms. Mahogany did not like that man to save her life. The very sound of his voice irritated her like nails on chalkboard. Mahogany constantly asks herself within her mind. "How can she be satisfied with a man like that?" "How can she keep taking him back after disappointment after disappointment?" Shari did not know herself worth. This was the example she set for her daughter's when it came to companionship (generational curse). Time went on dealing with the same old thing, day in and day out, year in and year out. In order to keep the piece around the house and nosy neighbors out of their business. Shari voluntarily gave Damian money to support his habit. It was too late for that because their marital issues traveled fast and the people in the community rejoiced at their marital flaws. How can you keep something like that hid? It's impossible. Time had past and Mahogany was now thirteen years of age and she felt like it was the highlight of her life. Mahogany's confidence was on an all time high. Mahogany made it into her seventh grade year at Charles Heights Jr. High School. Mahogany's daily schedule consist of band, basketball and church drill team. Shari needed extra income in order to keep up with the bills, extra curricular activities and other miscellaneous things. Shari went without in order for her girls to have. The income from Freedom Nursing Home did not bring in enough money to take care of the family needs and wants. Shari took on a second job working for Fort Autom Independent School District driving the school bus for the special need students. Shari work schedule began at 6:00 am and ended at 5:00pm. When Shari finished her bus routes, she went to her second job Freedom Nursing Home. Shari signed up for as much overtime as she could in order to come out ahead. Sharron was now eight years old attending Smith Elementary School across town which required her to ride the bus because it was beyond the two mile radius. Sharron bus arrived at 6:30 am sharp every morning and it was Mahogany's responsibility to make sure Sharron was properly dressed, fed and on the bus on time. Mahogany's bus did not arrive until 7:15 am every morning. Mahogany began feeling a bit under the weather that morning but she went to school regardless of how she felt. Mahogany did not believe in missing school. Mahogany liked the fact of being away from home to mingle with her friends. The second period bell had rung and Mahogany fell seriously ill and was sent to the nurses office by Mrs. Johnson her History teacher. The nurse took Mahogany's temperature and discovered that she had the symptoms of the flu. The school nurse called Shari and told her that Mahogany needed to go home immediately due to having the flu. Shari took off early, picked up Mahogany from school and nursed her. The sun rose on the next day and the flu had taken a toll on Mahogany. Mahogany took an absence from school until she was well enough to return. Shari allowed Mahogany to stay home because she was at the legal age according to the law to look after herself without parental supervision. Mahogany dreaded with everything within her that Damian was there because he was too lazy to find a job. Damian did not believe in the word job. Damian had it so easy he had everything at his finger tips. Damian had his own personal government assistance from home. No application needed. Damian received free rent, free food, free money, free medical attention and transportation services. Nothing was wrong with him physically. He was well capable of maintaining a job. Mahogany loved the fact that he was tucked away in his room until sleep wore off. Damian opened up the room door with his clothes in his hands and went in the bathroom as if he was preparing to go out and do something productive. Mahogany hummed to herself making up lyric's about him leaving and her having the house all to herself. "Mahogany is everything alright and why are you not at school." "I have the flu." Mahogany replied. Damian told Mahogany that he will be back later because he needed to take care of some business. Mahogany cracked a hidden smile at the thought of being alone and watching videocassette tapes on her new VCR player that her mother replaced from the one he had stolen. Mahogany's alone time was short lived. Damian came back drunk from consuming over the legal limit of alcohol. Damian for the life of him could not walk or stand straight. Damian knocked down everything that was in his path. Mahogany sick in her body got up and picked up after him like an adult cleaning up after a toddler. Everything he knocked down Mahogany put it back in it's assigned place. Damian stopped, turned around, looked at Mahogany breathing out funk that was strong enough to put anybody in a coma. "So you think your grown now picking up after me?" Mahogany paid his sarcastic comment no mind. Damian asks her the question again. "So you think your grown cleaning up after me?" "No I don't. I am just making sure this house stay in order because if mom come home and see this, she will be....." Mahogany cut if off realizing she did not owe a drunk man an explanation. Damian mumbled and wobbled unable to keep his balance. "Oh she's not going to do anything." Mahogany could not take it anymore, she had enough of the skunk breath. Mahogany went back into her room and started back watching her movie. Damian looked at Mahogany in a strange way letting her know that he was the adult around the house. The look that he gave her looked all too familiar. The look he gave her took her back to that place that she suppressed and convinced herself that it never happened. Mahogany was nervous and it showed. The spirit of molestation consumed him and convinced him that he could take what he wanted. Damian held Mahogany's arms over her head with his right hand and took off her pajama pants with his left hand, cupped her body against his and he took her as his own. Mahogany cried out but he silenced her with a blow to the head with his fist. Mahogany was in so much pain from the hit, the only thing that came out of her mouth was a silent cry. When the spirit of molestation was satisfied, it released him and went back into hiding. Mahogany could not believe that she walked for the second time through *"The Valley of Molestation."* A little time had passed and Shari called home from work to check on Mahogany. Damian knew that it was Shari checking in on Mahogany. Damian coached Mahogany on what to say before picking up the phone. Damian drew his face so close to Mahogany's face he could have seen the back of her tonsils. Mahogany told her mother that everything was good and there was no need to worry. Shari with a sign that everything was okay, hung up the phone and went about her workday. Mahogany with a blank stare on her face listened to the dial tone and slowly hung the phone up. Damian excused himself out of Mahogany's face and walk away stating that she better not come in-between him and his wife's marriage by revealing what he had done. Mahogany complied with his wishes and locked what he had done to her, in her mind and heart.

# CHAPTER SIX

## *The Valley of a Suicidal Mind*

The demonic spirit of suicide paid Mahogany a visit giving her two options to either run away from home or commit suicide as a way of escape. "What is the point of living?" The suicide demon whispered to Mahogany. Immediately, the devil showed Mahogany a vision of a rope with her hanging from it allowing it to strangle her to death. "Mahogany grab a bottle of pills out of the medicine cabinet. Take them all and it will make you forget about your problems." The suicide demon whispered to Mahogany. Mahogany almost succeeded with the offer of suicide until Sharron popped up in her mind. Mahogany did not want Damian to hurt her little sister the same way she had been hurt. Mahogany looked at the clock and at 3:00 pm sharp when Sharron banged on the door. Grandma Casity would have met her but Mahogany took the liberty to watch after her since she was home. Mahogany moving in slow motion, fixed Sharron a snack and went back to her room in silence. Mahogany watched Damian's every move making sure that her sister was safe from harm. Shari arrived hours later yawning, rubbing her hurting feet and exhausted from working two jobs. Mahogany wanted to tell her mother what her husband had done, but the spirit of fear consumed her and kept her silent. In the late night hour while

Mahogany laid in her bed wide awake surrounded by a dark room. The demon of fear and doubt visited her again. This spirit tampered with her mind reminding her that if she spoke up about what Damian had done, it will cause another family dispute. The devil kept tugging on Mahogany. "No one believed you then when it first happened. Why would they believe you now?" The demonic spirit of lies and deceit jumped in and whispered in her ear. "You have one purpose and one purpose only. You was put on this earth to be used for sex and kept a secret." Mahogany in a state of vulnerability fed into the fear, lies and deceit of the enemy. Mahogany gave into what the enemy told her because it seem as though they were right thus far.

A week went by and Mahogany was still hurt and confused about her life. Shari went about her daily routine leaving for work at 6:00 am and Sharron was on the bus by 6:30 am. Mahogany waited because her bus did not come until 7:15 am. Mahogany had a little time before leaving for the bus. Damian knew everyone's schedule like clock work. Damian came into Mahogany's room took her as his own and once again Mahogany traveled *"The Valley of Molestation."* Mahogany became immune to being Damian's sex toy and at times Mahogany enjoy it because it started to feel good to her. The spirit of lust overtook Mahogany and she began operating in the spirit of Jezebel, allowing it to seduce her mother's husband and the man she knew as step father. A year later something happened to and within Mahogany. Mahogany woke up with an I am not going to take anything off of anybody attitude. Damian picked the wrong day to approach Mahogany with his sexual desires. Damian began kissing on Mahogany but something within her did not want to walk the valley of sexual immorality (adultery) with her step father anymore. Mahogany stood up for herself, pimped slapped him with the palm of her right hand and Damian backed off. The hit from the palm of her hand was so hard it could have made a permanent tattoo on his face. Damian never bothered her again sexually. Mahogany gathered courage and strength to fight back. A year later Mahogany finally mustered up the strength to tell her mother the big secret. Shari asks Damian about the sexual encounters with Mahogany but as expected, he denied it. Shari could not believe that her daughter walked through this valley again. Shari called Damian's mother and told her what her son had done. To Mahogany's surprise she did not take up for him. Mahogany knew that since the big secret had been revealed, surely, her mother was going to kick him out for good. Shari swallowed the pill of betrayal and let Damian stay, even though all of the dirty laundry had been exposed.

## Spiritual Food for Thought

*2 Corinthians 1:8-10 states: 8 For we would not, brethren, have you ignorant of our trouble which came to us in Asia, that we were pressed out of measure, above strength, insomuch that we despaired even of life: 9 But we had the sentence of death in ourselves, that we should not trust in ourselves, but in God which raiseth the dead: 10 Who delivered us from so great a death, and doth deliver: in whom we trust that he will yet deliver us;*

## Spiritual Food for Thought

*2 Corinthians 12:9 states: 9 And he said unto me, My grace is sufficient for the: for my strength is made perfect in weakness. Most gladly therefore will I rather glory in my infirmities, that the power of Christ may rest upon me.*

## Spiritual Food for Thought

*Isaiah 41:10 states: 10 Fear thou not; for I am with thee: be not dismayed for I am thy God: I will strengthen thee;*

*yea, I will help thee yea, I will uphold thee with the right hand of my righteousness.*

## Spiritual Food for Thought

**Psalms 118:17** states: [17] I shall not die, but live, and declare the works of the Lord.

# CHAPTER SEVEN

## *The Valley of Masturbation and*

## *Thoughts of Lesbianism*

### *Self Dialog*

There is an old familiar saying that says "When a teenager reach a certain age they began to smell themselves meaning (no one can tell me anything). It's something about becoming a teenager that make one think that they are grown and have the answers to everything. Teenagers think that parents do not have the capability to understand their generation. I know, because I once was the teenager that thought this way about my parents. I thought my parents were outdated and could not comprehend today's issues that teens face. I had just turned 14 and thought I had it going on for myself. I dressed very well and cut off all of my long hair into a cute short hairstyle that worked well with the shape of my face resembling a new start.

## *Spiritual Food for Thought*

*Ephesians 5:3-5 states: 3 But fornication, and all uncleanness, or covetousness, let it not be once named among you, as becometh saints; 4 Neither filthiness, nor foolish talking, nor jesting, which are not convenient: but rather giving of thanks. 5 For this ye know, that no whoremonger, nor unclean person, nor covetous man, who is an idolater, hath any inheritance in the kingdom of Christ and of God.*

Mahogany boarded the school bus knowing that she looked good. The boys praised her and flocked to her like birds on bird food. The words of amateurs made Mahogany blush in a way that was undeniable. Mahogany liked the attention she received from the opposite gender. Mahogany did not see any harm in flirting. Besides, it was innocent with no intentions on taking it any further. Mahogany heard rumors traveling around school like the Egypt plague from her male peers about certain girls who they had been involved with sexually. Mahogany swore to herself that she would never become a headline in their conversation. Mahogany made a vow to herself that she will never put herself in those kinds of situations. Mahogany thought to herself that becoming pregnant at a young age was silly and just plain careless. Mahogany often wondered what it would be like to be in a relationship with the opposite gender but Shari kept her busy in extra curricular activities. Mahogany had no time to invest in a relationship. Mahogany schedule was as long as a broker firm meeting schedule. Besides, Mahogany could not allow herself to detour from the well mannered young lady that the public eye saw and spoke so highly of. However, behind closed doors there was another side to Mahogany that she did not want anyone to know about because of the shame and guilt that she felt in practicing such sin. Mahogany *"Walked through the Valley of Masturbation."* Mahogany found other ways to relieve the lust that throbbed within her. Mahogany was controlled by this unclean spirit called masturbation.

Masturbation became apart of Mahogany's daily tasks. Mahogany could not wait to be alone at home so she could use every bit of her energy to masturbate because she liked the sensation it gave her when it was time to explode. Mahogany liked when that spirit of masturbation rose up in her. Mahogany let that spirit take her without a rebuttal or a fight. Mahogany could not deny that she had forfeited her rights to have self-control to the spirit of masturbation. The spirit of masturbation had a stronghold on Mahogany that she could not shake off. The spirit of masturbation controlled her like a zoo keeper controlling an animal, moving off of every word that is being dictated. Mahogany did not need the physical man to do what she could do all by herself. Mahogany masturbated two or three times a day until it became harder for her to arrive to her final destination. Mahogany allowed her mind to travel to a place that she did not know was hidden in her. Mahogany began thinking about the body of a woman. The more Mahogany thought about it, the more she was turned on by it. The thoughts of being with another woman sexually gave Mahogany the motivation she needed to pleasure herself. Mahogany discovered that she had a hidden lust and desire for women. Mahogany knew that it was a sin that God hated. A matter of fact He gave this sin a name (abomination). Same gender sexual attraction was the reason God destroyed Sodom and Gomorrah with fire. Mahogany wondered if she encountered this spirit through incest when the males and females in her family seduced her. Mahogany was confused. She loved the fact of being with a woman but the feeling of being with a man was much stronger. Mahogany never mustered up the boldness to date or become sexually involved with a woman so she made love to them in her thoughts. Mahogany **"Walked the Valley of Masturbation & Thoughts of Lesbianism"** for many years because she carried around the access weight of an *"Uncircumcised Heart."* There came a time in Mahogany's adult life when she got tired of walking this valley. Mahogany prayed and fasted for days, weeks and months at a time in order for the demonic spirit of masturbation and lesbianism to release her. One day the spirit of masturbation and thoughts of lesbianism approached Mahogany but she fought and denied her flesh. It was then Mahogany saw and felt that which held her in captivity, pull out of her body bringing forth deliverance.

## Self Dialog

The spirit of masturbation and same sex desires right today are running rapidly spreading through every gender and nationality from old to young. People have lied on God making bold statements that the Lord made them homosexuals and lesbians. The Lord does not go against his word. Why would the Lord call it an abomination if He agreed to such sin? Why did God burn up the city of Sodom and Gomorrah with the people in it who committed this sin, if He agreed with such sin? The devil have even taken the rainbow sign that God made with the people, promising to never flood the earth again with water and tuned it into the national anthem and flag of the homosexual and lesbian community. I fought with the sin of masturbation and lesbianism. I'm not proud of what I have done, but I have to be real to help somebody. When you masturbate you are harming yourself. God did not create Adam to be alone so he could masturbate, he created Eve to explore and enjoy. Before I got delivered from this spirit. I took the very jewel that God created for my husband and defiled it by masturbating because I was too anxious and selfish to wait until God had joined my husband and I in marriage. Even now, while I am married. The enemy tries to test me with masturbation to see if I am weak enough to defile myself when my husband and I have a disagreement and my hormones are raging. The enemy comes in different ways, but with the same stuff; but the power of God that's within me rebuke, bind and deny the flesh reminding the enemy, that is not who I am anymore. God did not create Eve to be with Evelyn or Adam to be with Abraham. He create man and woman to enjoy each other in marriage and become fruitful. Homosexuality and lesbianism is not the natural order of God. God took the rib out of Adam and created his wife Eve (a woman). The nations are sleeping with an ancient demon that have misconstrued the mind to thinking that this is the way of living and it's acceptable in

Gods eyes. The devil is a liar!!! If Jezebel could return from the dead. I'm pretty sure from what she know now about hell. She would come back repenting and tell those who are committing sexually sin without any care in the world, to repent. If the people of Sodom and Gomorrah that participated in sexual sin could return from the dead. I'm pretty sure from what they know now about hell. They would come back repenting and tell those that are running around committing sexual sin without any care in the world, to repent.

## *Spiritual Food for Thought*

*James 1:14-15 states: 13 Let no man say when he is tempted, I am tempted of God: for God cannot be tempted with evil, neither tempeth he any man: 14 But every man is tempted, when he is drawn away of his own lust, and enticed. 15 When when lust hath conceived, it bringeth forth sin: and sin, when it is finished, bringeth forth death.*

## *Spiritual Food for Thought*

*1 Peter 2:11 states: Dearly beloved, I beseech you as strangers and pilgrims, abstain from fleshly lusts, which war against the soul;*

## *Spiritual Food for Thought*

*Leviticus 18:22 states: 22 Thou shalt not lie with mankind, as with womankind: it is abomination.*

## Spiritual Food for Thought

***Romans 1:18-28*** *[18] For the wrath of God is revealed from heaven against all ungodliness and unrighteousness of men, who hold the truth in unrighteousness; [19] Because that which may be known of God is manifest in them; for God hath shewed it unto them. [20] For the invisible things of him from the creation of the world are clearly seen, being understood by the things that are made, even his eternal power and Godhead; so that they are without excuse; [21] Because that, when they knew God, they glorified him not as God, neither were thankful; but became vain in their imaginations, and their foolish heart was darkened. [22] Professing themselves to be wise, they became fools, [23] And changed the glory of the uncorruptible God into an image made like to corruptible man, and to birds, and fourfooted beasts, and creeping things. [24] Wherefore God also gave them up to uncleanness through the lusts of their own hearts, to dishonour their own bodies between themselves: [25] Who changed the truth of God into a lie, and worshipped and served the creature more than the Creator, who is blessed for ever. Amen. [26] For this cause God gave them up unto vile affections: for even their women did change the natural use into that which is against nature: [27] And likewise also the men, leaving the natural use of the woman, burned in their lust one toward another; men with men working that which is unseemly, and receiving in themselves that recompence of their error which was meet. [28] And even as they did not like to retain God in their knowledge, God gave them over to a reprobate mind, to do those things which are not convenient;*

## Spiritual Food for Thought

***Genesis 19:1-28*** *states: And there came two angels to Sodom at even; and Lot sat in the gate of Sodom: and Lot seeing them rose up to meet them; and he bowed*

|63|

*himself with his face toward the ground; 2 And he said, Behold now, my lords, turn in, I pray you, into your servant's house, and tarry all night, and wash your feet, and ye shall rise up early, and go on your ways. And they said, Nay; but we will abide in the street all night. 3 And he pressed upon them greatly; and they turned in unto him, and entered into his house; and he made them a feast, and did bake unleavened bread, and they did eat. 4 But before they lay down, the men of the city, even the men of Sodom, compassed the house round, both old and young, all the people from every quarter: 5 And they called unto Lot, and said unto him, Where are the men which came in to thee this night? bring them out unto us, that we may know them. 6 And Lot went out at the door unto them, and shut the door after him, 7 And said, I pray you, brethren, do not so wickedly. 8 Behold now, I have two daughters which have not known man; let me, I pray you, bring them out unto you, and do ye to them as is good in your eyes: only unto these men do nothing; for therefore came they under the shadow of my roof. 9 And they said, Stand back. And they said again, This one fellow came in to sojourn, and he will needs be a judge: now will we deal worse with thee, than with them. And they pressed sore upon the man, even Lot, and came near to break the door. 10 But the men put forth their hand, and pulled Lot into the house to them, and shut to the door. 11 And they smote the men that were at the door of the house with blindness, both small and great: so that they wearied themselves to find the door. 12 And the men said unto Lot, Hast thou here any besides? son in law, and thy sons, and thy daughters, and whatsoever thou hast in the city, bring them out of this place: 13 For we will destroy this place, because the cry of them is waxen great before the face of the Lord; and the Lord hath sent us to destroy it. 14 And Lot went out, and spake unto his sons in law, which married his daughters, and said, Up, get you out of this place; for the Lord will destroy this city. But he seemed as one that mocked unto his sons in law. 15 And when the morning arose, then the angels hastened Lot, saying, Arise, take thy wife, and thy two daughters, which are here; lest thou be consumed in the iniquity of the city. 16 And while he lingered, the men laid hold upon his hand, and upon the hand of his wife, and upon the hand of his two daughters; the Lord being merciful unto him: and they brought him forth, and set him without the city. 17 And it came to pass, when they had brought them forth abroad, that he said, Escape for thy life; look not behind thee, neither stay thou in all the plain; escape to the mountain, lest thou be consumed. 18 And Lot said unto them, Oh, not so, my Lord: 19 Behold now, thy servant hath found grace in thy sight, and thou hast magnified thy mercy, which thou hast shewed unto me in saving my life; and I cannot escape to the mountain, lest some evil take me, and I die: 20 Behold now, this city is near to flee unto, and it is a little one: Oh, let me escape thither, (is it not a little one?) and my soul shall live. 21 And he said unto him, See, I have accepted thee concerning this thing also, that I will not overthrow this city, for the which thou hast spoken. 22 Haste thee, escape thither; for I cannot do anything till thou be come thither. Therefore the name of the city was called Zoar. 23 The sun was risen upon the earth when Lot entered into Zoar. 24 Then the Lord rained upon Sodom and upon Gomorrah brimstone and fire from the Lord out of heaven; 25 And he overthrew those cities, and all the plain, and all the inhabitants of the cities, and that which grew upon the ground. 26 But his wife looked back from behind him, and she became a pillar of salt. 27 And Abraham gat up early in the morning to the place where he stood before the Lord: 28 And he looked toward Sodom and Gomorrah, and toward all the land of the plain, and beheld, and, lo, the smoke of the country went up as the smoke of a furnace.*

# Self Dialog

Let's touch and agree in prayer. The spirit of sexual immorality I command you to come out right now in the Mighty Name of Jesus! I command you to loose possession over his/her mind, heart and soul right now! I send the spirit of the Holy Ghost now to burn up every perverted thought and action right now in the Name of Jesus! You spirit of Jezebel and Sodom & Gomorrah I stand in authority and command you to decay and exit out of their family lineage right now in the Mighty name of Jesus! I command the spirit of lust, masturbation, homosexuality and lesbianism to stand down and come subject under the power and Mighty Hand of God! Lucifer you cannot and will not bring them to hell with you for your time of control, lies and deceit has come to an end in Jesus Name! I declare and decree that every man, woman and child that is dealing with these sexual sins will repent and turn from their wicked ways! I declare and decree that from this day forth, that you will walk in freedom and never return to your old sinful self! I declare and decree that you will present your body as a living sacrifice unto the Lord! Now walk in your healing and deliverance for it is so, in Jesus Name. Amen.

# CHAPTER EIGHT

## *The Valley of Fornication*

The season of Summer had made it's entrance. The sun shined bright, the soft breeze of the air blew through the screen door, birds chirping in harmony and the bluebonnets bloomed through the ground with it's radiant color of blue, proudly representing the Texas state flower. Mahogany embraced summer but the thought of summer vacation being wasted from boredom did not set well her. Mahogany only summer activity was preparing for the church drill team competition in Phoenix, Arizona at the Convention Center. Mahogany went outside to enjoy Summer at it's fullest. The streets filled with people meeting up with their clicks, giving dramatic hand shakes, laughing, talking loud and brainstorming on how they were going to spend their day. Mahogany looked around and saw her best friend coming to keep her company. Tonya a lot like Mahogany could only go to certain places because of their parents rules and restrictions. Tonya and Mahogany set on the porch and made conversation about everything they laid their eyes on, despising their friends utilizing their freedom. "Mahogany, it's boring over here. Do you want to come to my house?" Tonya said in hopes of Mahogany seeing things her way. Mahogany agreed making her aware that her visit will be short because of drill team practice.

Mahogany's mind drifted on her up coming trip to Phoenix, Arizona. Mahogany could not wait to leave Texas. This trip had everyone's adrenaline pumping because of all the different churches that traveled from all over the United States representing their pastor and the state they lived in. The battle of the bands had nothing on the battle of the church drill teams. Churches came together in one place to spread the gospel of Jesus Christ through singing and quoting scriptures while stepping fraternity and military style, hoping to win first place, in order to take home the trophy and a year of bragging rights. Mahogany bounced back from drifting off about the trip that will soon take place and focused on her current situation with Tonya. Tonya and Mahogany found themselves doing the same thing they did at Mahogany's house. "Mahogany walk down the street with me." Mahogany out of curiosity. "What's down the street?" Tonya leaned over and whispered, "Timothy." "Really!" Mahogany said with excitement. Mahogany was well aware of the gentlemen Tonya spoke of. Mahogany knew of him, but not on a personal level nor did she really hold a conversation with him. Timothy was well mannered, well groomed and played football. Tonya and Mahogany strolled down the street and as soon as they stepped foot on his lawn, Timothy stepped outside, closed the screen door behind him, surprised at the company that stood before him. Mahogany could not resist the fact that Timothy made her smile. Timothy and Mahogany made eye contact and things became awkward between them. Mahogany looked around the enormous sized porch for a place to sit and saw both chairs had been occupied by him and his eldest brother whom happen to be def. Tonya stood on the steps and Mahogany stood on the porch a couple of feet away from Timothy, leaning against the chipped wood that outlined the porch. "What are you all up to?" Timothy asks. "Nothing, just bored." Tonya and Mahogany said in unison. "Bored huh?" Timothy confirmed. Mahogany shook her head in agreement to his response. Timothy and Mahogany locked eyes once again, as if they were the only ones on the porch. "Mahogany have a seat." Timothy offered with a generous smile. "Where am I going to sit? Both seats are taken." Timothy looked at

Mahogany. "Right here in my lap." Mahogany mind said "No" but against her better judgment her actions said "Yes." Mahogany set on his lap and noticed that Timothy had become aroused by her sitting on him. Mahogany looked at Tonya and raised her eyebrows as a hint that something was going on with Timothy. Tonya gave Mahogany the strangest confused look. Mahogany looked down as a guide to her mystery. Tonya took a deep breath, covered her mouth and chuckled. Mahogany felt something shoot through her that she had never felt before. Mahogany had become aroused by Timothy. Timothy felt and saw how relaxed Mahogany had become and took hold of their moment as an opportunity of a life time. "Do you want to go in the house." Timothy whispered in Mahogany's ear. "Yes" Mahogany answered with no intentions on taking it back. Mahogany looked at Tonya, but Tonya looked away with such disappointment in her decision to go in the house. Mahogany followed Timothy in the house. "I can't chicken out now." Mahogany played in her mind. Timothy took Mahogany to his room and for the first time in Mahogany's life she willfully gave her body up to someone that she liked. The spirit of fornication took them both until it was satisfied, and when done, it released them and went into hiding. Mahogany's lustful desire had her **"Walking through the Valley of Fornication."** Mahogany pressed for time, left, went home, cleaned up and headed to drill team practice. Mahogany ran down the street and over the railroad tracks making it just in time for the line up. What Mahogany did not know, is that her and Timothy irresponsible decision to have sex, gave them unexpected responsibilities. The church left for Phoenix, Arizona Saturday evening. Mahogany enjoyed the fun they had after working so hard to get the routines down perfectly. After a week in Arizona they packed up and headed home exhausted and without a trophy and bragging rights. A month had past and Mahogany noticed that her cycle had not come. Mahogany did not tell Shari because of the fear of knowing what she had done. Mahogany did not know that her mother had already noticed the unopened tampon package. Shari was on point when it came to the affairs of Mahogany. Out of nowhere the big question came. "Mahogany have your cycle came for this month?" Mahogany swallowed with a lump of nervousness in her throat. "No ma'am, not yet." Mahogany did not want to go through the remainder of the summer dealing with her mother nagging her about what was going on with her body. The only way she knew to avoid her mother's watchful eye was to call her father and ask if her and Sharron could stay with him for the remainder of the summer. Mahogany dreaded staying with her father because her and Sharron was not genuinely accepted by his new family. James agreed, picked them up, dropped them off, leaving them in the house alone with his wicked new family. A couple of days had passed and boredom took a toll on Mahogany until she saw this smooth caramel skinned, naturally curly haired, gorgeous eyed male walking on the sidewalk going in the apartments across the street from her father's house. Mahogany saw people from the surrounding areas taking their children for a swim where he lived. Mahogany dressed herself and her siblings in the appropriate swim attire and took her brother and sister by the hand and boldly walked across the street knowing that she was about to enter into a pool that she did not have legal access to because it was for residence only. Mahogany pressed forward with the anticipation of cooling down from the overbearing back to back 100 degree weather. Mahogany stepped into the pool embracing the coolness it brought to her body. Mahogany took a deep plunge into the water and when she came up for air she saw him. The guy she saw walking along the sidewalk was standing outside of the pool gate staring at her. Mahogany got out of the water, dried herself off and laid back in the body sized pool chair. He walked around the pool gate making his way to the other side to make conversation with Mahogany. "Hi, my name is Brian." "Hi Brian, my name is Mahogany." Silence came between them and Mahogany rolled her eyes beneath her sunglasses. "Are you from around here Mahogany?" No, I live in Fort Autom I am here for the summer visiting my father who live across the street at Benton Town Homes. "Oh, okay. Can I come and visit you sometime?" Mahogany took a deep breath. "Sure, why not." The date and time of his visit had been settled and the thought of him with her in her father's house made her blush. Mahogany knew that early mornings would be perfect because her father and step mother would be well on their way to work and her brother and sister would still be upstairs sleeping. Besides, Mahogany knew that her father would not approve of her having company over of the opposite gender. The following day Brian paid Mahogany a visit as planned. Mahogany was quite pleased on how their time together turned out. Mahogany extended him another visitation but this time she gave him the invitation to come on a daily basis as long as it was early during the day. Mahogany loved Brian's company and the non-sexual conversations that struck up between them. There were no signs of a hidden agenda but what they shared in the last couple of days showed nothing more than a genuine friendship, so Mahogany thought. Two weeks had past and Brian and Mahogany had became well acquainted with each other. The room became still and the spirit of lust came over them and they adventured each other sexually and after the spirit of lust was satisfied, it released them and went into hiding. Once again Mahogany *"Walked through the Valley of Fornication."* Immediately, Brian put on his clothes and left out of the door as fast as he came in the door. Mahogany stood on the porch awaiting to see if Brian would come back with some kind of explanation on why he rushed out of the house, but there was no trace of him anywhere. Mahogany gave up and while reaching for the door knob she saw Brian walking passed her on the sidewalk, ignoring her as if they had never met or said two words to one another. Mahogany felt embarrassed, low and degraded. Here it is, the person she liked, held multiple conversations with, had written her off after they had been sexually involved with one other. Two days had passed since Mahogany's encounter with Brian. Mahogany set on the porch fussing at herself for allowing herself to go there with Brian. Mahogany heard talking and laughing from a distance then it got closer and closer. Mahogany could not believe what her eyes were seeing. Brian, the guy she just had sex with was walking down the sidewalk talking and laughing with his arms around the waist of another chick. Mahogany decided that she was not going to approach him, beat herself up or have a pity party any longer because she knew better. She set her self up for disappointment. Mahogany could not blame anybody but herself. Mahogany made her bed, so therefore, she had to lay down in it. "Even a prostitute have enough sense to not give up their cookies for free." Mahogany said out loud. Mahogany was in trouble. Mahogany's chose death from an uncircumcised heart due to premarital sex.

## Self Dialog

Fornication is when two people are not married having sexual intercourse. Fornication is the most common sin that the enemy uses to kill, steal and destroy. Fornication comes to kill because many have died from AIDS/HIV. People have gotten sexual transmitted diseases, some curable and some are not curable. How many people have lost their lives by guns, knives, fist fights and suicide because so and so slept with someone's girlfriend or boyfriend? How many demons have entered into you and the people in this world through fornication? When you are fornicating with someone, your sleeping with the 4 or 5 demons they have from sleeping with other people. How many lives have been destroyed through ungodly soul ties due to fornication? How many families or individuals have the spirit of fornication destroyed due to school drop outs from early pregnancy, depression, bitterness and isolation? How many virgins have fornication broken? How many children are being raised up in a single parent household because of fornication? How many men and women are in the prison system because of fornication? Last but not least. How many people are burning or going to burn in hell because of fornication? Enough said.......

## Spiritual Food for Thought

***Ephesians 5:6-12*** *states:* ⁶ *Let no man deceive you with vain words: for because of these things cometh the wrath* *of God upon the children of disobedience. 7 Be not ye therefore partakers with them. 8 For ye were sometimes darkness, but now are ye light in the Lord: walk as children of light: 9 (For the fruit of the Spirit is in all goodness and righteousness and truth;) 10 Proving what is acceptable unto the Lord. 11 And have no fellowship with the unfruitful works of darkness, but rather reprove them. 12 For it is a shame even to speak of those things which are done of them in secret.*

## Spiritual Food for Thought

**Psalms 51:10** *states: Create in me a clean heart, O God; and renew a right spirit within me.*

# CHAPTER NINE

## *The Valley of Rejection*

The sky grew dark and the light from the stars covered the sky. Mahogany turned off the television, walked into the laundry room, grabbed the flower patterned comforter, set on the couch in her father's living room, fluffed her pillow and drifted off listening to the clock singing the tic-toc national anthem. The Lord put Mahogany in a deep sleep and took her into the spiritual realm of prophetic dreams. Images played in Mahogany's mind as though she was watching a movie in a downtown cinema. Mahogany saw herself in an auditorium standing before thousands of people wearing a white robe, holding a microphone in her hand, preaching, praying and laying hands as the spirit of the Lord fell upon them bringing healing, deliverance and salvation. Instantly, Mahogany woke up speechless and puzzled about what the Lord had shown her. Mahogany glanced at the clock and noticed that it was 3:00 in the morning. The house became very quiet and still like when Mahogany heard a sweet calming voice. "Preach." Mahogany searched around the living room for this voice that spoke to her, but she found no one. It dawned on Mahogany, that the voice she heard was that of Gods. God spoke to her for the second time. "Preach." Mahogany thought surely, God had her confused with someone else. God rebuked Mahogany in love. God reminded her that her temple belongs to Him. "Oh...my. God is in my father's living room." Mahogany said to herself. Mahogany in a state of shock was a bit confused about this voice that reached out to her. Mahogany laid down and pondered on her encounter with God. Sleep found Mahogany and she drifted off into a deep sleep. God appeared to her again the same morning in her dream. Mahogany saw herself preaching in a bigger place, wearing a white robe, holding a cordless microphone in her hand, standing in front of thousands of people; but this time she stood on stage without having to lay her hands on anyone, because the spirit of the Lord consumed her and by her standing there all kinds of infirmities were healed, souls were delivered and set free. The Lord revealed to Mahogany that when she come before His people, no matter the warfare they are dealing with, the Lord was going to reveal himself through her. God came to tell Mahogany that the Apostolic, Prophetic, Evangelism and Healing mantle was upon her life. Mahogany pondered on what God had revealed to her; but the truth of the matter was, in her mind, she was not ready. Mahogany did not want to answer or surrender to her calling at a young age. Mahogany felt as if she had her whole life ahead of her. Mahogany battled back and forth within her own self. "I am far from ready to preach to Gods people." "Shoot, I can't even preach myself out of my own mess." Mahogany barely cracked the bible open, when she did, it was out of feeling obligated to do so. Mahogany decided that she wanted to do what she wanted to do, regardless of what God revealed to her. Besides, church took up too much of her time. Bible study on Wednesdays, youth choir rehearsal once a month on Thursdays, drill team practice twice a week, BTU every other Saturday at grandmas and service on Sundays. Mahogany believed in the Lord and His word, she just wasn't ready to submit and live by them. Mahogany wanted to have fun and live her youthful life. Mahogany wanted the call from God to leave her alone. Little did she know, no matter what she did or where she went, that voice was going to tug on her. Mahogany could not deny that God consumed her in her dreams and that she was spiritually on fire from preaching. She just was not ready to give up the flesh. "God is calling me at a young age." Mahogany thought aloud. Mahogany wanted to be like the rest of the teens her age mixing and mingling with other people. Instantly God took Mahogany down memory lane when she spoke His word in front of the congregation in youth pageants and how God consumed her and manifested himself through her. Mahogany remembered many telling her that she have a calling on her life and she was anointed to preach the word of God. Mahogany cracked a smile at the thought of surrendering but the spirit of fear, guilt, excuse and doubt visited her and convinced her that she was not ready to answer the call and all the responsibilities that came with it. "What in the world could God possibly want with someone like me?" Mahogany stated. Mahogany mind set on the fact that her heart was too sick and heavy with sin. Mahogany knew she had been displeasing in the eyes of God, but he still called her. Mahogany thought  long and hard about what God asks her to do. Mahogany went with her own will, rejected Him and turned a def ear to God. Mahogany wanted to fit in with the rest of the world. After all that God had done for her, she walked away. He rescued her time and time again and this was how she repaid him. Mahogany liked being a wretch undone. Mahogany liked being the dog that returned back to it's vomit. Mahogany pleaded with God in hopes that He would never bother her again. Mahogany chose death and *"Walked through the Valley of Rejection"* due to the hardness of her heart, which brought forth disobedience.

# *Self Dialog*

When you disobey God, expect trouble to find you. Disobeying God caused me to walk in the wilderness longer than I had to. My wilderness period was not forty years like the Israelite's when they disobeyed God, but it sure felt like it. I encountered trouble for years because I did not want to submit. Some of my troubles was just life, but a lot of my troubles was due to disobedience. It's one thing I found out. Since I did not come in voluntarily. I came in involuntarily walking through a long cold valley. Obedience is better than sacrifice (1 Samuel 15:22). I sacrificed a lot.

## Spiritual Food for Thought

**Proverbs 26:11-16** *states: ¹¹ As a dog returneth to his vomit, so a fool returneth to his folly. ¹² Seest thou a man wise in his own conceit? there is more hope of a fool than of him. ¹³ The slothful man saith, There is a lion in the way; a lion is in the streets. ¹⁴ As the door turneth upon his hinges, so doth the slothful upon his bed. ¹⁵ The slothful hideth his hand in his bosom; it grieveth him to bring it again to his mouth. ¹⁶ The sluggard is wiser in his own conceit than seven men that can render a reason.*

## Spiritual Food for Thought

**Matthew 21:16** *states: ¹⁶ And said unto him, Hearest thou what these say? And Jesus saith unto them, Yea; have ye never read, Out of the mouth of babes and sucklings thou has perfected praise?*

# CHAPTER TEN

## *The Valley of Teenage Pregnancy*

## *(A Baby Having A Baby)*

Mahogany did not tell a soul about her visitation from God. For the first time, Mahogany enjoyed every bit of the overdue father and daughter time. Mahogany in awe of her father's capability to take on the duties of an activities coordinator without the help of anyone. James marked his calendar with scheduled picnics at the park, a night at the movies, swimming and basketball. Mahogany knew that somewhere in the midst of James planning, basketball had to be apart of the fun. James thought he was the next Michael Jordan except he missed every time, hitting nothing but pure air. For a brief moment Mahogany mind drifted from the family fun and thought about how this moment was bitter, sweet because summer vacation was coming to an end. The month of August had approached and it was time to return to the excessive loud alarm clocks, overwhelming school work and after school activities to flood her day. Sharron and Mahogany packed up and said their farewells to summer fun. Mahogany found herself reminiscing about her summer vacation until she arrived in front of the white and blue framed house she called home. Mahogany resented that house because of all the bad experiences she encountered with her step father. James got out of the car, grabbed a hand full of heavy luggage and escorted Sharron and Mahogany up the walkway that led to the elegant decorated porch. James stood on the porch and told Sharron and Mahogany that he loved them and hoped their summer vacation met their expectations. Sharron and Mahogany cried and hugged their father as if it was their last time seeing him. Shari ran to the door with so much joy in her eyes that her girls made it back home. "So, how did your summer vacation go with your father." Mahogany must have been excited as well because the first thing that came out of her mouth was the visitation from God in her dreams. Mahogany told Shari that God had something for her to do. Shari looked at Mahogany with a smile as if she had received confirmation of what she already knew. Shari spoke gracefully in so little words. "I know baby....." Shari explained to Mahogany that what God had shown her was a glimpse of what is to come. Shari explained to Mahogany that God had given her bits and pieces of the plans that he has in-store for her. Mahogany took a deep breath and thought about the road that lies ahead. After the conversation about her visitation from God, it became silent. Mahogany waited for her mother to drill her about her cycle, but instead she delighted in preparing dinner. Mahogany went into her room prepared for school thinking about what tomorrow may bring. Mahogany was officially an eighth grader. Mahogany spotted some of her friends, sat at the cafeteria table and waited for the school bell to ring. In the midst of the congested on going traffic in the cafeteria Mahogany caught eyes with Timothy. Timothy went about his business and Mahogany went about her business disregarding the chemistry between them. They spoke to each other from time to time but only on a friendship basis. Timothy prepared for football season and Mahogany was too involved in her studies and after school activities. Social time did not fit into either of their over booked schedules. Mahogany decided to drop band and focused on track and basketball. Mahogany looked forward to track season. Mahogany loved competing and striving to break the school record. Try outs begun and

Mahogany ran giving it everything she had to seek the approval of the track coaches. Mahogany expectations was high. Mahogany expectations was to run the fastest and jump the longest distance. The coaches was very pleased in Mahogany's running time. Now she had to meet the requirements for the long jump. Mahogany ran with every bit of strength and energy she had in hopes of superseding her previous record in the long jump. Mahogany head felt light and her body became weak as if it was going to give out on her at any moment. Mahogany faintly jumped and disappointment came over her knowing that she fell short of reaching her goal. Mahogany felt nauseated and exhausted. Mahogany got up and dusted herself off adjusting her shorts and shirt that rolled over her belly during the jump. Mahogany noticed that her shirt was tighter than usual. Mahogany thought she had picked up one of her team mates shirts and put it on by accident. Ms. Heathner the athletic teacher looked at Mahogany in the strangest way as she walked off the training field holding her stomach. Mahogany thought to herself. "Here we go, she's staring at my body." The look she gave Mahogany made her feel very uncomfortable. The rumor around school was that Ms. Heather did not want a husband and neither did she have or want children. She had the reputation of being a lesbian and wearing it proudly. What Mahogany did not know is that Ms. Heathner had no interest in little girls whatsoever, but upon examining her stomach it looked a little abnormal to her. Ms. Heathner left the training field, went into her office and closed the door. Mahogany knew that her chances of making the team was over. Mahogany barely functioning throughout the school day managed to pull through. Mahogany thought that whatever bothered Ms. Heathner must had worked itself out on it's own. The school bell rung for dismissal and the hall ways flooded with loud, overbearing, immature students, throwing their books in their locker, preparing to board the bus. Mahogany boarded the bus in silence and remained silent the entire ride home. Mahogany pondered on what could have puzzled Ms. Heathner; it bothered her that she did not know. Mahogany got off the bus and saw her mother's car parked in the driveway. Mahogany scrunched up her face because this was out of the norm for her mother to be at home this early because she drove the school bus. Mahogany walked in the house and found her mother anxiously waiting for her in the living room. Mahogany stepped two feet into the house when her mother demanded that she put her stuff down and get in the car. Mahogany felt as if she was going to have an anxiety attack. Mahogany thought to herself. Mom did not even say "Hello, How was school? Or anything" Here it was. The moment she thought she had dodged, hunted her. Shari looked at Mahogany with piercing eyes. "You better not lie to me. Did your cycle come?" Mahogany looked at her mother with so much hurt, knowing that she was about to disappoint her in ways she never imagined. Mahogany signed and with resentment. "No ma'am, I have not." Shari broke the news down to Mahogany that she scheduled a doctor's appointment to see what was going on in her body. Shari looked at Mahogany again; but this time more serious than the first time. "Mahogany, I am going to ask you a question and I better get an accurate answer." Mahogany shook her head in agreement to her mother's wishes. "Have you been having sex?" Mahogany looked at her mother crazy as if she had been offended by an annoying stranger. "Mom no!" "How can you accuse me of doing something like that?" "I am not having sex!" Mahogany went into defense mode, knowing that everything was about to crumble before her eyes. "Okay." Shari said in a sarcastic voice as if she knew that her lies was about to seek her out and swallow her whole. "Were here Mahogany, get out of the car." Mahogany nerves began to scramble making her sweat glands kick into overdrive. Mahogany knew that she had unprotected sex with Timothy before going to Phoenix, Arizona but she still insisted on holding on to the lie to the very end. Mahogany wished she could have avoided this doctor's visit for a few more months. Shari checked-in at the front desk and at that point, Mahogany knew that there was no turning back. This was it, Mahogany thought to herself. "I am about to see Dr. Redman and he is about to expose my secret." Mahogany loved Dr. Redman. He was nice and a very handsome man indeed. Mahogany knew that after he expose her, she was no longer going to love him or think that he was still handsome.

Mahogany knew that she was going to hate him for being the barrier of bad news. Dr. Redman assistant nurse opened the door. "Mahogany Stallone!" She greeted Shari and Mahogany and led them to a vacant examination room. The nurse began probing Mahogany with questions about when was her last period and personal things about her body. The answers Mahogany gave did not line up with the questions that were asks and it made the nurse look at Mahogany in a distrusting way. Mahogany thought that she could out smart the nurse who went to school to become a professional in Women Wellness. "Well…..Mahogany, I am going to take a sample of your urine and then I need you to change into this gown for examination." The nurse walked out and left Mahogany and her mother alone. Shari and Mahogany did not pass a single word to each other. It was dead silence for 15 minutes. Dr. Redman came into the room and greeted them with his luring smile. Dr. Redman looked at Mahogany and began asking her more annoying questions about her sex life; but of course, she denied it. "Lay back Mahogany so I can examine your breast and abdomen." "I am going to apply a little pressure and tell me if you feel tender or pain." Dr. Redman was not born yesterday and neither did he become a doctor on yesterday. Mahogany knew that Dr. Redman knew that she was with child. This is what he do for a living. Dr. Redman felt around Mahogany's stomach applying pressure to her pelvic and breast, hitting all of Mahogany's tender spots making her move in defense mode accompanied by a frown of pain on her face. Dr. Redman looked at her, took his gloves off and raised his eyebrows at Mahogany. Mahogany looked down acknowledging what that look meant. Dr. Redman grabbed his chart with Mahogany's life changing results. Dr. Redman looked at Shari and then looked at Mahogany. "Do you want the good news first or the bad news first?" "Good news." Mahogany was anxious to hear the good news. Dr. Redman proceeded with her life changing results. "Well Mahogany, the good news is that you do not have any fluids building up in your stomach causing your stomach to swell." "The bad news is your six months pregnant." Mahogany began calculating back and discovered from May to November was six months. Mahogany could feel her mother looking at her with such disappointment from the corner of her eyes but Mahogany disregarded making eye contact because she could not bare the disappointment and shame she had brought upon herself and loved ones. Mahogany got dressed, took her prescription for prenatal pills and made her next appointment. Shari let Mahogany have it as soon as they pulled out of the parking lot. Shari never fussed at her the way she did that day. Mahogany cried, remembering the vow she made to herself by not becoming pregnant at a young age, falling prey to the discussion of her peers hot topics. Mahogany bit her own words. The question Mahogany had been waiting for finally surfaced. "Mahogany, whom have you had sex with and what is his name?" Mahogany dreaded answering her because she was already at the verge of an anxiety attack. Mahogany did not want to mention Timothy from her hometown. For some stupid reason Brian came out of her mouth. Mahogany knew that there was no possible way that Brian was the father. Mahogany lied because she was embarrassed to be the baby momma of someone in her hometown. Mahogany used the excuse that Timothy would deny ever being with her. Everyone in her past denied her. Besides, Timothy did not pay that much attention to Mahogany after their sexual encounter. Shari pulled over at Warren's gas station around the corner from Dr. Redman's office. Shari did not drink alcohol but after the news she just heard Mahogany thought she may have stopped to purchase an alcoholic beverage. Instead, Shari went to the pay phone. "Who is she calling on the pay phone when she have a phone at home?" Mahogany heart leaped through her shirt at an accelerated rate when she discovered that the person her mother called was her father. Mahogany reading her mother's every word and gesture from inside of the car wanted to take out running as far as she could go with no intentions on returning. Shari accused James of being a reckless and negligent father to the point that their daughter had to result in sex to pass time. James did not understand why she was so mad at him. "Why are you fussing at me Shari, she is down there with you?" "I'm fussing because she got pregnant while spending the summer with you." Shari motioned for

Mahogany to get out of the car to speak with her father. Mahogany going in for the kill, put her ears to the phone and endured every word of frustration that came from her father's mouth. Mahogany understood her father's agony so she listened without saying a word. She understood that his baby was having a baby. Mahogany felt the shame that she had brought upon her parents. Her father pastured his own church. What kind of example did she set? Here it is her father is preaching about sustaining from sex and his own house is out of order. Who want to obey a pastor who's children rebel against the very word that he preach to others? Mahogany was one out of many that made the saying "Preacher's kids are the worst ones." come to reality. James demanded to know the young man whom had relations with his daughter. Mahogany hesitated to tell her father out of fear of what he may do. Mahogany younger brother listening to James conversation with Mahogany blurted in the back ground. "I know where he live." James picked up Mahogany to pay Brian a visit. James rung the doorbell and Brian's mother greeted them with a smile that flowed gracefully. "Yes, may I help you?" James with an attitude and angry look on his face blurted out in disgust. "Is your son home?" "Yes, is everything alright?" Brian mother responded with so much meekness. James took anger to another level. "No, he got my daughter pregnant!" Grace went out the door when she heard James words. Brian's mother pulled her glasses down to the tip of her nose, threw the newspaper down that she obliged in on the end table and glued her eye's to Mahogany's stomach. "Brian get out here now!" Brian scared for his life, looked at his mother and saw Mahogany standing at his door step. "Do you know her Brian?" To Mahogany's surprise Brian admitted that he knew her. Brian's mother invited them in and the conversation began. Brian could not deny being with Mahogany because her nosy brother had seen them around each other. The conversation of the when, why and where went in a merry-go-round for two hours getting nowhere. Both parents shouting at each other and towards Brian and Mahogany did not make the situation any easier. Time was well spent and what seem like an on going storm had finally calmed. They rushed out of the house and headed back to Fort Autom. "Shari can I speak to you outside on the porch for a minute?" James asks with a squeak in his voice. "We need to come up with another plan because she cannot have this baby. Mahogany ear hustling heard every word that came out of their mouth. Mahogany heard the word abortion. Abortion was not an option to Mahogany. Mahogany did not like the fact that her mother and father did not include her in such an important decision. Mahogany did not agree with her parents planning her baby's funeral. It was her poor decision to have sex, so now she has to deal with the consequences on dealing with *"A Baby having A Baby."* Shortly after receiving the news about being a soon to be mother her stomach blew up in a matter of weeks. Mahogany did one of the hardest things she ever had to do in her life. Mahogany dropped out of all extra curricular activities. Mahogany went to school and back home. Her daily routine was set on repeat. Even though this was a vulnerable time for her, she embraced the support from her immediate family and church family. Mahogany pregnancy gave her a great deal of attention. Mahogany got whatever she wanted from fast food to clothes. Mahogany pregnancy rode on smooth waves that went in her favor until the spirit of guilt and shame consumed her. Mahogany went down memory lane when she spoke a mighty word at the youth pageant. By favor of the judges she became queen of Ms. El Bethel Baptist Church. She remembered the exact title she spoke on "Breaking the Yoke." How embarrassing and humiliating to be crowned queen of the church and pregnant with child. "Oh my, this was not the kind of example I wanted to send out to the youth." Tears formed in Mahogany's eyes as she looked down at her fat stomach loaded with stretch marks resembling a road map signifying that her body will never look the same again. Shari had a little surprise of her own to cheer up Mahogany's mood. Shari and the members of the church gathered in secret to surprise Mahogany with a baby shower. "Mahogany I am hungry. Do you want to go get something to eat?" Shari knew that turning down food was nowhere on Mahogany's list of things to decline. Mahogany mouth watered thinking about what she was going to put on her plate first and then second. Shari pulled out of the drive way and took a right turn instead of a left turn going in the opposite direction of food. Shari drove over the railroad tracks, slowly applied the breaks, pulled up in front of the church and turned the engine off. "Get out." Mahogany looked at her mother confused, mad and hungry; wondering why her mother stopped everywhere else but to food. "Mahogany get out. I have to do something and it's going to take a minute, so I need you to get out of the car." Mahogany followed her mother through the side door that led straight to the youth ministry and fellowship hall. "Surprise!!!" Mahogany eyes bucked and her mouth dropped like an army man dropping from a jet. Mahogany covered her mouth with the palm of her hand surprised at the many people that came together to plan a baby shower for her and her unborn child. Mahogany leaked tears of joy as she scanned the room looking at the people that came out to celebrate the new life that will soon enter this world. Mahogany could not believe what her eyes beheld. Members of the church, family and friends surrounded the wall from corner to corner surrounding the tables of food and gifts that set in the center. Tears poured down even harder when Mahogany looked up and saw all of the elegant decorations that coordinated well with the Mickey Mouse theme she wanted for her baby. The expression on Mahogany's face showed that she was forever thankful and grateful for the people that was apart of her life. They could have condemned her but instead they supported her through it all. The month of February came and everyone anticipated the day that her baby would arrive. Mahogany went to church which happened to fall on Valentine's Day. Mahogany stomach cramped up and she alarmed her mother that she was in need of assistance. Shari rushed Mahogany to the hospital were she stayed for hours under evaluation until the doctor discovered that it was a false alarm. Ten days had past since her false encounter with labor pains. Mahogany fixed herself some breakfast and as she was getting ready to enjoy it, a sharp pain hit her stomach, making her drop everything that was on her fork. Shari left a couple of emergency numbers for Mahogany to call in-case she was out of reach. The first person that was accessible to call was Auntie Beverly. Beverly called Shari informing her that her grand baby was on the way. Shari excited about the new edition to the family, took off of work and came to her daughter's aid. Shari grabbed Mahogany's tote bag, turned on the emergency blinker lights and drove as fast as she could to Charleston's Hospital. All Mahogany could think about was her son and getting back into her favorite jeans. Mahogany endured thirteen hours of labor before delivery. July 19, 1993 a son was born unto Timothy and Mahogany. He came in this world making a grand entrance letting everyone know through his signature cry that he had arrived. Dr. Redman announced that it was a boy and that he weighed 7lbs and 19 inches long. Mahogany held her son and named him Darrius. Mahogany wrapped her mind around the fact that she was a baby cradling a baby in her arms. Instantly, Mahogany went from adolescence to adulthood. Darrius and Mahogany was released from the hospital five days after her admittance. Dr. Redman had a day off so Dr. Chatuwanage discharged the both of them. Upon coming out of the electronic door of Charleston hospital; it dawned on Mahogany that her motherly duties have now kicked in full time. Mahogany nursed Darrius at home for six whole weeks. The allotted time for leave of absence from school had expired and it was time for Mahogany to return to school for the remainder of the school year. Mahogany passed and excelled with honors to the ninth grade. Mahogany was now a student of Cranbar High School as a full time student and parent. Mahogany needed a part time summer job to take care of the needs of her new born son. Mahogany found employment with the assistance of JTPA working at the recreation center collecting fees for swimming pool attendees. Mahogany loved her job because it was three blocks away from where she lived. Mahogany's schedule consisted of working, coming home and attending to her son. Summer came to an end and so did Mahogany's job. Mahogany ninth grade year begun. Mahogany enrolled Darrius into the Cranbar childcare program. Mahogany took Darrius to school and dropped him off at the daycare that was attached to the back of the high school allowing teenage mother's to be responsible and finish school. Mahogany did not like depending on her mother to do everything for her so she decided to get a job while going to school. Grandma Casity picked Mahogany up from school, dropped her off at work and kept Darrius until Shari got off of work. Mahogany relieved at the fact that Darrius was safe at Grandma Casity's because her cousin Jack went to prison for charges of molestation of another minor. This was the best time of Mahogany's life. She had Darrius in her life and Shari finally kicked her husband Damian out and divorced him. Shari allowed Mahogany to be a teenager and enjoy doing what she loved to do. Mahogany reunited with the church drill team and tried out for color guard. The color guard coincide with the band at half time on Friday night at the football games. Mahogany without a doubt made the team. Mahogany finished high school within three years instead of four. Mahogany recovered after having to repeat the third grade twice. Mahogany went to summer school when she could and received enough credits to be a senior in high school in order to graduate with her right class. Mahogany did not have the privilege of getting out early her senior year because she worked hard juggling both Jr. and Sr. classes together for two semesters. Mahogany enrolled herself into Perriville College to pursue her life long dream as a paralegal. It was something about law that fascinated her. Cranbar High School Board Committee granted Mahogany with a 1,000 dollar scholarship towards her college education for all of her hard work.

## *Self Dialog*

I was truly a baby having a baby. I had a lot of support, but I still took on unnecessary responsibilities at a young age. Here I was a baby myself taking care of a baby. I was fourteen when I had my son. I love my son and he is the joy of my life but my heart beat for the mind of these teens today. I have ran across girls that think that by trapping a man by getting pregnant will make him stay. I have ran across teens that think they have made a big accomplishment because they are having premarital sex. Teen are bragging and walking around proud like that is something big. Somehow, teenage pregnancy have become a fad or the in thing to do. Having a baby is not a walk in the park and taking care of one is not the easiest journey. I encourage every teen to practice abstinence until marriage. Enjoy your youthful life and everything that it brings. I want to encourage the young teenage mother's to keep going and continue your education. Look at me. I did it. I had a baby at the age of fourteen, graduated from high school, held down a job, went to college and graduated. I am an author, entrepreneur and operate in ministry. Anything is obtainable as long as you put your mind to it. You are more than a sex symbol. You are smart, radiant, courageous, unique and beautiful. Don't let anyone tell you any differently because you had a child at an early age. You can do it. You are the doctor that you said you are going to be. You are the pediatrician that you said you are going to be. You are the CNA/ Certified Nurses Assistant that you said that you was going to be. You are the lawyer that you said that you are going to be. You are the law enforcement that you said that you are going to be. You are the CEO, CFO, manager or supervisor of a company that you said you are going to be. You are the entrepreneur that you said that you are going to be. I declare and decree that you will make your mark in this world and become great in whatever you want to do because lying on your back, having babies, staying on welfare, struggling and raising kids alone is not your portion. You are somebody. So get up from that stinky thinking and start new with a new way of seeing things. Young teenage woman and young teenage man, make it count. You are the future for tomorrow and a door opener for the next generation to come. I did it, so will you.

## Spiritual Food for Thought

*Galatians 6:9 states:* [9] *And let us not be weary in well doing: for in due season we shall reap, if we faint not.*

# CHAPTER ELEVEN

## *Though I Walked Through*

## *The Valley of the Shadow of Death*

Mahogany turned eighteen years of age. By law she was now recognized as an adult. Mahogany started a new chapter in her life. The new chapter in her life was tested and tried. Mahogany was now able to make decisions on her own without parental consent whether good or bad. Mahogany set in her favorite spot under the tree, laid back in the off white lawn chair that her mother bought from Home Depot. Mahogany closed her eyes for a second, tilted her head back and embraced the breeze that swept against her strawberry stuffed face, allowing an article in Ebony Magazine take her away on an African Safari. Mahogany's moment of solitude was interrupted when she noticed that she caught the attention of a gentleman by the name of Rashad Hamilton. Mahogany did not know him all that well, but she did know that he was well know around the neighborhood. Rashad drove around the same block four times watching her before gathering the strength to approach her with confidence. Rashad's approach towards Mahogany was direct and straight to the point. "I have liked you for sometime now. Will you go out on a date with me this Saturday night?"

Mahogany felt as if she had reached the top of the world. Mahogany was graduating on Friday from her senior year in high school. "Why not celebrate my graduation this Saturday by letting him take me out." Mahogany reasoned within her own mind. Mahogany evaluated Rashad from top to bottom. He appeared to have all the characteristics that she desired in a man. Rashad carried himself well, drove his own car and work an 8 hour job. The only flaw Rashad had according to her was the fact that he was in his late 20's still living at home with his mother. Mahogany gave Rashad her final response and agreed to let him take her out to dinner. Rashad smile, nodded his head up and down surprised at Mahogany's immediate response. Very well then, I will pick you up at 8:00 pm. Mahogany agreed and Rashad excused himself so Mahogany can get back to enjoying her magazine. Friday May 23, 1997 @ 7:00 pm, Mahogany walked proudly across the graduation stage receiving her high school diploma. Mahogany screamed and shouted with joy because she had accomplished what many of her classmates that had children did not. Mahogany entered a new chapter in her life. At that moment, Mahogany wrapped her mind around stepping on campus during the Fall semester attending Perriville College located in Perriville, Texas. Mahogany went home after graduation and prepared for her night out with Rashad on Saturday night. Rashad pulled up in his Cadillac at 8:00 pm as promised. Rashad wined, dined and treated her as though she was the princess he had been waiting for his entire life. Mahogany gave into his charm and let him shower her with gifts and acceptable intimacy. To pass time by Mahogany allowed herself to get wrapped up in Rashad's world. Mahogany and Rashad shared the same interest and they became inseparable. The evening flowed perfectly with dinner, laughter and a movie. "This is a special celebration. Let's make a toast to our love for one another." Mahogany turned towards Rashad, scooted to the edge of her seat, ecstatic about toasting to their instant love. "It doesn't get any better than this." Mahogany thought to herself. Mahogany summer break was over. Mahogany packed up and left for Perriville College to pursue her dream of pursuing law. Rashad did not let the distance between them stop him from seeing her. Rashad faithfully picked Mahogany up every weekend from college to make up for the time lost during the weekday. Rashad pulled into One Stop liquor store after a night of whining and dining. Mahogany expected a bottle of champagne. To her surprise he purchased a bottle of Coca Cola and a bottle of liquor called Hennessy. Rashad went to his trunk that so happen to have a chest full of ice. Rashad prepared Mahogany a drink and then prepared a drink for himself. For the first time Mahogany was introduced to alcohol. Mahogany waited for some type of instructions from Rashad on the do's and do not's of drinking alcohol. Mahogany took her drink and drunk it like she had been drinking for years. "That wasn't so bad. Pour me another?" Rashad took her cup, filled it with Coca Cola and alcohol and handed it to Mahogany. Mahogany took her drink and owned it. Rashad knew Mahogany had exceeded her alcohol limit. Rashad looked at Mahogany and began laughing at her sluggish and incomplete sentences. "Hey Mahogany, let's get a motel room for tonight, so we can sleep off this alcohol." Mahogany agreed to Rashad's proposal because it made since. Besides, she did not want her friends to see her intoxicated. Rashad pulled up at the entrance way of Camelot Inn, paid for their motel room, got in the car and saw that Mahogany was passed out sleep. Mahogany put her life in the hands of someone she only had known for a little while. The following morning Mahogany woke up dizzy and with a terrible headache. Mahogany looked down and saw that her arm and legs had red bruises on them that had not been there before. Mahogany for the life of her could not remember how it happened. "Mahogany you consumed too much alcohol and lost your balance hitting the rail on the stair case." Rashad explained. Mahogany looked at her arm and legs again and immediately a red flag went up. "Um, Rashad honey, the marks on my arm and legs do not look like I hit or fell down anything. These marks look like someone abused me." Mahogany believed his lie and overlooked any possibilities of what could have happened because she did consume a lot of alcohol. In the state of intoxication the one she called boyfriend and lover beat her. What Mahogany thought was love made her blind to the truth. The more Rashad came around, the more of him started to show. Mahogany returned to school the following morning and did not whisper a word about what happened to her. Mahogany kept it in a safe box within her heart. Mahogany tucked her arms in her shirt hiding the bruises from her roommate. Mahogany was happy to know that she had dodged interrogating questions because her roommate was still sleep. Mahogany went to class the next morning and after class her roommate met her in the hallway and told her that Rashad waited for her in the parking lot outside of their dorm room. "Why isn't he at work?" Mahogany said underneath her breath. Rashad made a habit of popping up at her school unannounced to see if he could catch her in the act of doing something he would disapprove of. Rashad insecure ways made him jealous. Rashad's jealousy began to override him like a high tide overshadowing a surf board rider. Mahogany questioned Rashad's employment amongst herself. "How can a man work an 8 to 5 job during the week and take off at the drop of a hat without any consequences of losing his job?" On her way to meet up with Rashad she stopped by the court where she met up with a couple of friends on a daily basis. Mahogany was excited about introducing her friends to Rashad. They knew she had someone in her life, but she never had a chance to introduce them. Rashad looked at Mahogany laughing and carrying on with her friends as they approached his car. Mahogany introduced her friends to Rashad and he greeted them with an unwelcoming half smile. Rashad engaged in the conversation and told a joke from time to time, making a good impression on Mahogany's friends. When all of the talking and laughing had ceased, Mahogany hugged her friends and told them that she will catch up with them later after she spend some alone time with her man. Rashad looked at Mahogany from inside the car and spoke to her in such a gentle voice. "Get in the car. I want to take you out to lunch." Mahogany got in the car, closed the door and buckled her seat belt. Mahogany's heart softened by the sacrifice he made by losing money to come see about her well being. Mahogany reached over to show her appreciation to Rashad with a kiss, but the response she received in return was one she did not want or expect. Rashad bawled up his fist and punched Mahogany in the left side of her jaw. Mahogany took her right hand and held her jaw in disbelief of what just happened to her. Mahogany felt as though a 15 pound exercise weight had crashed in on her face. That was the moment that Mahogany came into realization that Rashad had abused her without any questions or hesitation. In a firm voice Rashad spoke to Mahogany as though he was the father and she was his child. "DON'T YOU EVER LET ME CATCH YOU WITH THOSE GUYS AGAIN!" Mahogany gave him a distressed look as she held her face. Rashad was jealous because there were two males in the mix among Mahogany and her friend girls. "Are you trying to tell me that I can't have friends...?" Rashad looked at her as though she committed a crime. "Mahogany, you know what I mean and I do not want to explain myself again." Rashad's behavior was foreign to her. Mahogany tried to comprehend what took place in his mind that it resulted to violence. The demonic influence of insecurity and high imagination consumed him and tricked him into believing that Mahogany was cheating on him. A war was going on within Mahogany and it stayed locked up inside of her because she did not have the courage to speak to anyone about it, so she confided in alcohol to help her cope with her struggles. Mahogany loved him too much to leave. Mahogany without even knowing it inherited another generational curse of alcoholism. Mahogany drinking habits became an under detected suicide waiting to happen. Mahogany abused alcohol and it transformed her into someone she did not recognize. Mahogany found herself angry all over again lashing out at anyone she felt wanted to hurt her in any kind of way except Rashad. This feeling Mahogany felt for him captured her and held her in captivity. Mahogany became selfish, thinking about nobody but herself at times. Mahogany played around with fire and entertained unclean spirits within her boyfriend and the one's that nested within in her. Mahogany dreaded the path she had taken in her relationship with Rashad, but blind love would not let her walk away. Mahogany ignored her self worth, looked danger in the face and lived in darkness. The generational curse of self worth took a toll on her. Mahogany saw her mother go through this same situation and now she have patterned after her footsteps. Rashad made a habit of beating and cheating on Mahogany time after time again. Rashad mood swing varied from day to day. When someone made Rashad upset he would take his frustrations out on Mahogany in private. Mahogany suffered so much abuse on a weekly basis she became immune to his punishment. Mahogany persuaded herself that the love he had for her equaled the same amount of love she had for him. Mahogany persuaded herself that Rashad's anger came out the thought of losing her. Mahogany did not want people probing into her business so she made up lies about how she got the bruises on her body to keep herself from looking embarrassed and stupid. Mahogany knew that the lies she told did not fool anybody. Inspite of what people said she should do, she chose to stay and defend her prosecutor. Rashad controlling issues revealed that something deeper was going on with him that he could not share with anyone, so he released it through negative behavior. The weekend had come and Mahogany yielded to his apologies. Rashad picked Mahogany up from school and told her he wanted to take her to Perriville Mall to buy her something nice to show how apologetic he was from his abusive behavior. Rashad parked his car and all of a sudden he snapped. Rashad got out of the car, opened her luggage and threw her clothes onto the mall parking lot and drove off leaving Mahogany stranded. Mahogany looked around with embarrassement from the people starring, gossiping and pointing fingers at her. Mahogany grabbed her clothes and personal hygiene bag and walked across the long field in the scorching hot sun, hoping for a cloud to shed some shade during her walk back to school. What was suppose to be a wonderful evening at the mall turned into a satanic outburst. Rashad physical, mental, emotional and verbal abuse affected Mahogany in ways she never imagined. Mahogany's slacked in her studies and turned her energy towards pleasing Rashad and alcohol. Regardless of what Rashad did to Mahogany, she still chose to *"Walk through the Valley of the Shadow of Death."* Rashad took pleasure in calling Mahogany everything but her birth name. Rashad wanted his cake and eat it to. Rashad's perfect world consist of a girlfriend slave with the benefits of flirting with other women, but yet she still chose ***death***. Fear would not let her walk away in-spite of their love hate relationship. Mahogany somehow managed to get through her first semester of college as a freshman. Mahogany packed up her things and went home for summer break. Rashad used this opportunity to gain more control over Mahogany. Rashad went apartment hunting because he felt that he owned Mahogany and she should be in the same house with him. Rashad found a two bedroom, one bath apartment. Mahogany went through unwanted advice from her family and friends about not moving in with Rashad, but she still chose ***death***. Mahogany's fury went to another level at the nerve of her family and friend's trying to give her counsel when their marriages and relationships drowned in defeat. "How dare they have the audacity to tell me, what was not of God, when they are shacking and fornicating." "How is it the blind want to lead the blind?" Mahogany focused on the possibility that things would change for the better. Rashad convinced Mahogany that he wanted to work on their relationship before blending their families together. Mahogany believed him and moved in with him for the summer. What Mahogany thought would be summer bliss turned into a severe thunderstorm. Rashad controlling behavior separated her from her own son through manipulation. Mahogany made arrangements for Darrius to stay with Shari through the summer. Mahogany put her boyfriend's needs before her own son needs. Mahogany rather baby set and meet the needs of a grown man who was capable of taken care of his own self.

## Self Dialog

What a very high price to pay just to say I have someone to love and cuddle with.

Mahogany could not believe it, Rashad did not just take his frustrations out on her, he also took his frustrations out on his own son Michael. Michael and Darrius was the same age. Spending time with Michael made Mahogany miss Darrius. Mahogany picked up Darrius to spend some time with him and to give her mother a break from a responsibility that was not hers to carry. After a long day of fun, Darrius fell asleep and Mahogany cradled him in her arms and carried him into Michael's room, laid him in the bed and tucked him in tightly. Mahogany rejoiced and thanked God for a peaceful day. Mahogany felt a little exhausted herself. Mahogany stood under the warm waterfall shower allowing Calgon to take her away and then off to bed she went. Rashad waited for sleep to find Mahogany with no signs of waking up anytime soon. In an instant the demonic influence of jealousy and anger took over him and he found himself in Michael's room standing over Darrius. Rashad hit him, threatened him and told him to keep silent. Out of fear Darrius honored his request and kept silent. The generational curse of fear and physical abuse came after her son. Mahogany did not tell her parents what happened to her out of fear and shame and now her son walked that same valley of fear and shame. Mahogany woke up the next morning and saw that the bottom of Darrius right eye was puffy. Rashad told Mahogany that his eye was like that when he woke up. Rashad evaluated the pillow Darrius slept on and came to the conclusion that the pillow may have caused Darrius to have an allergic reaction. Rashad's mother gave him the pillow so he called her to asks where she got it from. Mahogany believed him because he was so concerned about Darrius well being. Mahogany packed up Darrius things and drove him home to Shari. "Mahogany, what happened to Darrius eye?" Mahogany began to explain and suddenly Rashad interrupted her and took over the conversation telling his version of what happened to Darrius. Shari looked at Rashad with disgust letting him know that she knew that his story was smothered in lies. Shari became frustrated with Mahogany because she could not see past his lies and deceit. How could she see? She was too blind by what she thought was real love. Mahogany loved and ran after Rashad to the point it did not matter if it cost her everything she had, including her freedom. Rashad taught Mahogany how to run his drug business at home while he was gone to work. He taught her how to cook, cut up and make a profit of a drug that ruin lives on a daily basis. Mahogany took care of his in home drug business bringing in illegal money and performing all of the wifely duties. There was only one problem, they were not legally married. Rashad and Mahogany considered themselves married by common law. Mahogany grew up in an atmosphere of shacking and fornication and adopted the lifestyle. There were times Rashad acknowledged the efforts Mahogany put in on his behalf and treated her as if she was his queen and dared anybody to say anything different; and then after a week of pampering, Rashad mind and heart tucked back into it's shell of darkness and began treating her as though she was his worst enemy. Rashad did not care how much money Mahogany made for him or how much effort she put in preparing his meals, he still despised her. Rashad came home from work, slammed the door and immediately went off into a rage and scoffed at the food Mahogany prepared for him with love. Rashad rage rose because his boss had written him up at work for not making productivity in weeks. Rashad could not retaliate against his boss out of the fear of losing his job, so Mahogany became the perfect victim to take his place. The following afternoon Shari called Mahogany informing her that she was on her way to pick her up because there was something she wanted to show her. Shari pulled up, blew the horn and waited for Mahogany to come outside. Mahogany looked in the mirror hoping that her bruises did not look as bad as she thought. Mahogany got into her mother's car without saying a word. Shari saw the bruises on her daughter's body but kept silent. "What could possibly be so important that she had to come across town to get me?" Mahogany thought to herself. As they got closer to Shari's house Mahogany saw a 1993 red 4 door Dodge Shadow parked in her mother's driveway. Shari parked her car by the curb in front of her house, looked at Mahogany and asks her what she thought about the car parked in the driveway. "It's okay. I like it because it's small and seem reliable." Shari smiled with relief, went into her purse, pulled out the keys to the car and handed them to Mahogany. "Here, it's yours." Mahogany was lost for words.

Mahogany eagerly got out of the car in disbelief of owning her own car. Mahogany walked around her car pleased at what her eyes beheld, got excited, jumped up and down and ran over to her mother and hugged her tightly and with a loud voice. "Thank you mom!!!" Mahogany got in her car, drove off and waited for Rashad to come home from work to tell him the good news. An hour later Rashad came home and Mahogany jumped up with excitement and told him about the surprise her mother had given her. Rashad looked out of the window, shrugged his shoulders and grunted. Rashad despised the fact that Mahogany was mobile and no longer had to rely on him to take her where she needed to go. That was apart of his control to keep up with her whereabouts and to keep her dependent on him. Rashad gave Mahogany the silent treatment the entire day. The sun rose on the following day and Rashad went through his morning routine preparing himself for an 8 hour work day. Rashad grabbed his keys off the key rack and glanced at the keys that went to his lovers new car. The demonic spirit of control consumed him, took her keys and hid them before heading out for work. Mahogany woke up, washed her face, brushed her teeth and went about her daily routine as a common law house wife. Mahogany pleased at her outstanding cleaning skills, jumped in the shower, got dressed and decided to take her new car for a little drive around town to see how well it drives. Mahogany went to the key rack and discovered that her keys were gone. Mahogany thought she may have misplaced them so she searched the house thoroughly for her keys and could not find them. "Maybe Rashad picked them up by mistake on his way to work." Mahogany reasoned with herself. Mahogany went back into her room and pondered on where she might have laid her keys. Rashad called on is lunch break to check on Mahogany. "Rashad have you seen my car keys?" "No, why would I have your keys?" "I can't seem to find them anywhere. I thought I hung them up on the key rack." "Mahogany, that's why you don't need a car. You just got the car and you have already lost the keys." Rashad said in disgust. Rashad hung up in her face and the dial tone greeted her. Mahogany pondered on his words, confused about the disappearance of her car keys.

Mahogany wanted to asks Rashad if he had taken them on purpose, but out of fear for her life, she kept silent. Rashad came home from work and verbally abused Mahogany about losing her keys. Mahogany kept silent and went to their room and fell asleep. The sun rose on the following morning and Rashad went about his daily morning routine and left for work. Mahogany woke up, walked in the living-room and saw Rashad's socks and an empty plate on the floor. Mahogany opened the blinds and began picking up after his mess when the sun beamed through the window, shedding light on the tall stacked radio speakers by the entertainment. Mahogany saw something shining from within one of the speakers. Mahogany drew closer to the radio speaker and discovered that Rashad hid her keys. Mahogany wanted to leave, but yet she still chose *death*. Mahogany could not move and her heart and mind could not convince her that she was headed towards destruction. Rashad had Mahogany reeled in like a fish on a hook preparing to scrap off pieces of her identity. Rashad manipulated her with materialistic apologies. Mahogany lived in fear of the psychological hooks and knives that constantly pierced and hurt her. Rashad came home and noticed Mahogany was acting funny towards him. Mahogany did not look at him because of what he had done. Rashad looked in the speaker and noticed the keys were gone. Rashad turned to Mahogany allowing the spirit of anger to consume him. Rashad grabbed Mahogany, put her neck between his legs and squeezed until she gasped for air like a fish grasp for water when separated from it. Mahogany spoke to Rashad in a strained voice. "You say that you love me...., but your actions say you hate me." Rashad heard those words barely making it out of her mouth thought about what she said and released her from his grip. No matter how much Mahogany tried to please Rashad it was never good enough. Mahogany could not escape the darkness that haunted her. Mahogany tucked herself away in their bedroom and did not come out until the next morning. Rashad went to work and Mahogany decided to come out of the room to evaluate the list of things she needed before going back to school her sophomore year in college. Mahogany made it halfway down the list when she heard a familiar voice.

"Preach." Mahogany looked around the apartment but no one was in the apartment with her. It happened again. "Preach......" Mahogany thought that voice had left because it had been awhile since she heard it at her father's house. Mahogany ignored the familiar voice and chose *death*. Mahogany ignored God and declined her assignment. Mahogany turned a def ear to God, yielding to her own will and ways. Since then, things became very intensed in Mahogany's life. Instead of Rashad coming home from work, he stayed out as long as he could partaking in his secret agendas. Mahogany knew he was foul because she felt something abnormal going on with her body. The odor and irritation in her pelvic area was unbearable. Mahogany went to the clinic and received some disturbing news. Rashad had been sleeping around with other women and gave her an STD called Trichomonas. Mahogany did not want to be around other people because of the embarrassing smell. The doctor told her it was curable and prescribed her some penicillin to get rid of it. Mahogany took the pills for a day and stopped. Mahogany fought back and forth in her mind. "What good would it do to take these pills when I am going to sleep with him again and risk the chance of getting it back?" Mahogany did not tell Rashad that she went to the doctor because she knew that he would turn things around on her as if she was the one doing the cheating. "I have been faithful to him, treating him like a wife treat a husband and he goes out and have unprotected sex and I get a trip to the clinic." "How dare he!" Mahogany screamed at the top of her lungs in her secret place when no one was around. The betrayal that she felt resembled a wife that just found out that her husband cheated and discovered there's another child involved. Mahogany was a prisoner in her own home. She was being dictated on what to do, how to do it, when to do it and where to do it. Inspite of the tears, beatings, cheating, sexual transmitted disease and the headaches, she still chose *death*. Mahogany wanted to get out of it but did not know how. Mahogany slowly started to lose her mind behind closed doors wishing for a sign of freedom. Mahogany did not tell Rashad she was going to get a job. She begged him to let her have a job. Mahogany, a grown woman begging a man to make grown up decisions for her that she could have made herself, if she knew her self worth. Rashad agreed to Mahogany's plea out of greed. Rashad saw her money as his money to whine and dine other women. Mahogany trained at Wal-Mart in the sporting goods department. Mahogany worked a whole two weeks to get her first paycheck. Mahogany off day fell on payday, so she decided to pamper herself. Mahogany always dressed nice and kept her hair and nails looking good. Mahogany stopped by Dee's Nails Salon and waited to be serviced. As soon as Mahogany set down her beeper went off with a telephone number and 911 page from Rashad. Mahogany asks the nail technician if she could use their phone because it was a very important call. Mahogany knew how Rashad got when she did not answer his calls with haste. Mahogany dialed the number nervous and afraid of the monster that was about to answer the phone. "What are you doing?" Rashad asks. "I am treating myself by getting my nails done." Mahogany closed her eyes after she thought about what she said and wished she had kept her mouth closed. Rashad held the phone in silence and hung up in Mahogany's face. Rashad took a half day off of work claiming he was not feeling well. Mahogany almost jumped out of her chair when she saw Rashad entering the nail salon. Rashad watched Mahogany's every move hoping she mad eye contact with him. Mahogany dreaded the last process of getting her nails done because she did not want to face Rashad's fury. Mahogany paid the nail technician, squeezed a strained smile and walked past Rashad. Rashad gave her a displeasing look as if she should have consulted him first before doing anything. Mahogany knew a confrontation was arising, so she quickly went outside, pulled out her car keys and unlocked the door. Rashad followed Mahogany to the car, snatched her purse out of her hand and got in his car. Rashad dug through her purse and robbed her of all of her hard earned money that she worked hard for, leaving her twenty dollars. "How dare you come and take the money that I worked hard for in order to do what I want!" Mahogany shouted with a loud voice. Rashad did not use his mouth to speak. He spoke with his eyes letting her know that what she implied did not matter to him one bit and if he wanted to he will do it again. Rashad threw Mahogany's purse out of his car window, scattering everything that was sealed in it. Mahogany watched her cold hearted man drive off with her hard earned money. Tears streamed down Mahogany's face like a river. Mahogany picked up her purse, threw it in the passenger side of the seat and drove to her mother's house. Mahogany did not have anything else better in mind to do. Mahogany decided that she had enough. Mahogany pulled into her mother's driveway, rushed in the house and told her what Rashad had done. Shari disliked him because she knew he abused her daughter and he was nowhere near good enough for her. Shari looked at Mahogany, pointed her finger in her face and ran that I told you so speech to Mahogany, but she turned a def ear to every word that came out of her mouth. Mahogany did not want to hear about her bad choices. What she needed from her mother was comfort in the valley. Shari demanded that Mahogany go to the police station to file a police report. Mahogany got in her car and followed behind Shari to the police station. After filing the report, the reporting officer made it clear that there was really nothing they could do because of her involvement with Rashad. The chief of police began asking Mahogany questions about Rashad's personal affairs, instead of worrying about how to retrieve her money back. The chief of police inquired if both cars that Rashad drove belong to him. Rashad drove a burnt orange colored Dodge Ram that set low to the ground, with limo tinted windows, white wall tires that stuck out with gold rims and an expensive radio system that shook the trunk. Rashad second car had the same work done as the Dodge Ram except it was a Cadillac with a candy blue custom paint job. The officer asked if Rashad worked and Mahogany confirmed that he was a full time employee at Max Steel Warehouse. The officer asks if she noticed anything strange like an increase of income, but she lied and said she did not. The officer went deeper into their personal lives asking Mahogany if she lived with Rashad. Mahogany told the officer that she lived with her mother because she had made up in her mind that she was leaving Rashad and moving back home with her mother. Mahogany did herself a favor by not adding her name to the lease agreement just in case things did not work out. "Out of curiosity officer Why are you concerned with how Rashad is living?" Mahogany asks. "There is a lot of abnormal traffic going in and out of his apartment and that's why we have our eyes on him." Rashad loved flaunting his stuff around making others jealous of his lifestyle. Rashad's lavish lifestyle did not match up with the income he brought home from his job. Mahogany swallowed at the thought of being caught in a lie. Mahogany knew the correct answers to all of the officers questions; but out of fear she fell to come forth in truth. Mahogany nerves went out of control at the thought of accidentally selling drugs to an undercover cop and that was the reason he interrogated her. The officer shook Shari and Mahogany's hand and sent them on their way. Shari and Mahogany made it half way down the hall when he called out her name. "Ms. Stallone, be real careful." "Yes sir, I will." Mahogany replied. Shari and Mahogany parted ways. Mahogany made it home and twenty minutes later the phone rung. "Hello." "Um Mahogany, you know that phone that I gave you as a gift to take back to school?" "Yes." "Well, I am going to have to buy you another phone to take back to school because I am going to sell it to another woman who want it." Mahogany argued the point because it was a gift from him to her. This was no ordinary phone, it was unique and came with many features. Mahogany knew Rashad was lying. He did not want to sell her phone. He wanted to give it another woman as a gift from him. The conversation between her and Rashad got heated and they argued back and forth amongst one another trying to get each others point across. Mahogany had gotten tired of trying to get her point across to Rashad because he stood solid on his decision to sell the phone. "What is the point of arguing?" Mahogany said to herself. Mahogany hung up the phone and stomped around the house like a five year old kid. Mahogany packed up her clothes, shoes and all that belonged to her and stuffed her car to the fullest capacity, hardly leaving herself any driving room. Mahogany locked the apartment door, put the key under the doormat and left. Mahogany went to her mother's, unpacked her things and that's where she stayed for the remainder of her summer break. Rashad arrived home from work and saw that Mahogany and all of her stuff was gone. Rashad beeped Mahogany's pager constantly every two minutes as if it was a life or death situation. Mahogany stood firm in not responding to any of his calls. Rashad many attempts failed, so he called Shari's house phone. Shari snatched the phone cord out of the wall because the constant calling had gotten on her last nerve. The same night the narcotics team gathered, busted down his apartment door and raided it disturbing his sleep. They searched and found evidence of illegal substance laying out on the kitchen table and in his bedroom. The following morning Rashad made top news. Out of sympathy Mahogany went to visit Rashad in jail knowing that she won't see him again because she had to go back to college the following Monday. Mahogany set down and waited for Rashad to come out for visitation. Rashad set down and for the first time they talked to each other looking at him through a glass window that separated them. Rashad stopped in the middle of their conversation and looked at Mahogany and said. "The interesting thing that the officer ask me while searching the apartment was if a girl lived here." Mahogany knew of the officer Rashad spoke of. Mahogany knew immediately that Rashad thought she had gone to the police station and snitched on him. Mahogany drew close to the window and looked Rashad straight in his eyes without fear. "I did not expose your secret. God did!" Mahogany got up, hung the phone up and left. Rashad did not see her again until his court date. Awhile had past since Rashad had been incarcerated in Fort Autom county jail. Rashad court date had come and Mahogany missed her morning classes to be with his mother for support. The jury ruled in favor of the prosecutor and passed judgment on him that resulted in a guilty charge of possession of illegal substance and sentence him to six years in prison. Mahogany knew it was wrong to feel the way that she did, but she did not feel an ounce of sadness for him. Mahogany found peace and happiness. She was finally free. Mahogany went to the doctor and received treatment from the STD that Rashad gave her and in a few days, the penicillin healed her. Mahogany raised her hands in the air thanking God that the transmitted disease was curable. Mahogany returned to school and focused on her studies and the freedom that found her and her son Darrius.

## *Self Dialog*

God saved me once again. If the argument had not taken place about the phone, I would have been in Rashad's apartment caught in the cross fire when the drug squad arrived. I would have been serving some serious time in federal prison. Jesus knew the plans he had for me. Jesus came down to see about his lost bride. I played the harlot and cheated on Him, but he still loved me and shed mercy upon me. I was the run away bride; but the love that he has for me did not let the feelings of hurt and betrayal keep him from me. A matter of fact that made him come after me even more. Jesus came for me without second thoughts and rescued me. Jesus gave me another chance to repent and get it right.

## *Spiritual Food for Thought*

*Ezekiel 34:11-12 states:* [11] *For thus saith the Lord God; behold, I, even I, will both search my sheep, and seek then out.* [12] *As a shepherd seeketh out his flock in the day that he is among his sheep that are scattered; so will I seek out my sheep, and will deliver them out of all places where they have been scattered in the cloudy and dark day.*

## *Self Dialog*

It was by God's grace that I maintained my freedom, even though I was not faithful to Him and chose **death**. God still gave life to me and planned a way of escape for me even **"though I Walked through the Valley of the Shadow of Death."** I have gone through some death experiences that many men, women and children have committed homicide, suicide or lost their minds over going through what I went through. It was the grace of God and his hand of protection that kept me. In reality if God hand was not upon my life, it would have ended at an early age, buried six feet under ground. God sheltered me. God did not create us to be punching bags. Any kind of abuse whether verbal, physical, mental or emotional has absolutely nothing to do with love. Lives have been cut short due to abuse of all kinds. Jesus gave us life, so that means that He is the only one who can take life away. People of God we should love one another as Christ loves us.

After settling in her dorm room; Mahogany dressed to perfection wearing a long snap around the neck orange summer dress that flowed with her structure accompanied by gold accessories and open toed strap around high heel sandals that made her orange polished toes look extravagant. Mahogany set outside of her dorm room on the newly installed waterproof bench. The campus flooded with new and old students letting loose exploring the campus however they saw fit. Mahogany smiling within and without about the drama that dissolved out of her life. "Excuse me, are you alone?" Mahogany's eyes took hold to the handsome man that spoke to her. Mahogany couldn't help but notice the black fish net shirt he had on revealing every bit of muscle that was behind it. The glaze from the sun bounced off of him making his mocha skin tone stand out even more. "This man has class and dignity about himself and knew how to holla at a sista." Mahogany said within herself. He carried himself as a gentleman, dressed nice and kept his hair, beard and mustache well groomed. Mahogany felt as if she was going to melt at any moment. "My name is Jacoby." He grabbed Mahogany's right hand with grace and gave her a smile that said I walk confidence. Mahogany could not deny that he resembled that of a model from a fashion magazine. Jacoby was everything she desired in a mate. Jacoby went to church, pursued a higher education, cooked, cleaned, opened doors and he handled her gently and genuinely, taking time out to care about her well being. He knew how to hold her and he delighted himself in the things that interest her. They made their relationship official. The arousal from every sexual encounter blew Mahogany for a loop every single time. Strong feelings of love had developed from all of the time they had invested in their relationship. They stuck to each other like glue around the clock when homework did not overwhelm them. Mahogany never felt like this before. A matter of fact, he was too perfect. Mahogany twirled and danced in a world that she thought never existed. Jacoby took Mahogany away from all of her past hurt and pain. Jacoby took interest in Mahogany as a person and not for what she could do for him. He spoiled Mahogany's mind, body and soul. Mahogany thought God had favored her because of all she had been through. They knew they were soul mates and marriage was bound to be apart of their future. Jacoby and Mahogany dined, studied and worked out together on a regular basis making their bond stronger. What Mahogany felt was real love and not tainted. Mahogany did not have to live in fear around him. For a whole semester Mahogany experience his unchanging love for her. Jacoby and Mahogany spent Christmas and New Years Day waddled up in each others presence, counting it all joy that they have found each other. The second semester rolled in, bringing the change of season with it. Jacoby called Mahogany informing her that he was not coming back to school for the semester due to other obligations. Mahogany figured that the other obligations had something to do with money. Jacoby did not let that stop him from seeing Mahogany. He called everyday and drove an hour on the weekends just to be close to her. Time went on and somehow and someway, the calls and the visits slowed down drawing them further apart. Jacoby started working at Walters Warehouse. His job required him to work twelve hour shifts, while the study of law had Mahogany in the law library all day. A friend of Mahogany informed her that the real reason Jacoby could not come to Mahogany on the weekends was because he had gotten another girl pregnant. Mahogany heart crumbled when she heard the unbearable news that her too perfect boyfriend had betrayed her. Mahogany grabbed her chest from the pain that smothered her and cried with a loud voice. "I was suppose to carry his child, not her." "Jacoby led me on as if I was the only one in his world, only to find out, that it was a lie." Jacoby looked, talked, walked and dressed the part, only to find out that later he will be displayed as an imitation of Mr. Right. The fairy tale that Mahogany thought would never end, did. The man that Mahogany had grown to love was gone, disappeared without a trace. Mahogany went down memory lane every time the opportunity presented itself. Mahogany completed her sophomore and Jr. year at Perriville. Mahogany missed the love and the companionship that they shared. Mahogany longed for the time spent and the love that caught her by surprise. Mahogany wanted to feel that love again, so she accepted what she thought was love. Shortly after Jacoby and Mahogany unexpected break-up Mahogany fell into the arms of another. Mahogany began dating Ralph back in her hometown after her Jr. year of college. Ralph was fourteen years older than Mahogany. Mahogany went old school because she wanted to be with a more experienced man that have out grown childish games. Ralph showed interest, but something was missing and it was the word called love. Mahogany felt alone and empty inside because the love was not there. Once again Mahogany allowed the scales to shade her eyes blocking them from seeing the truth because she did not want to be alone. Ralph called all the time but hardly ever spent time with her. Mahogany stood out on her mother's porch admiring God's creation of the earth and everything in it when she saw Ralph riding around with another woman in his car, passing by her without even saying a word. Ralph must have had some kind of women code book on (How to Talk to other Women in Front of the One Your With) because the brotha was just that good. Ralph made all kinds of excuses to not answer the phone when one of his male friends called; but when a woman called Ralph thumb pressed the answer key faster than a rat eating cheese. Ralph covered up his mess with lies, assuring Mahogany that she have nothing to worry about, because the women he spoke to were long time friends of the family. Ralph told Mahogany anything to keep her quiet. The calls sound as if it might have been a midnight booty call made undercover. Ralph spoke in one word answers, yes, no and okay.

Mahogany thought to herself. "If she was just a friend of the family. Why come she have not met any of these so called friends of the family?" Ralph and Mahogany never spent time alone, other people was always involved. Ralph hung up the phone and told Mahogany he wanted to take her to his best friends birthday party to show her off. "Finally" Mahogany said within herself. Upon entering the birthday party Ralph walked off leaving Mahogany lost in the crowd to dance with other women. He lied, he did not even introduce her. Mahogany fought through the crowd on the dance floor, found a vacant chair and placed it beside the keg of beer and drunk until looking like the hind of a donkey no longer mattered. A man approached Mahogany looking every bit of fifty years old, took the cup out of her hand and swiveled her onto the dance floor. Mahogany got her groove on the floor and became the highlight of the party. Mahogany dropped it down to the floor and picked it back up again flowing with the rhythm of the music. Ralph did not pay attention to Mahogany until she shook her curves on the dance floor. Ralph and Mahogany's relationship should have been friends with benefits because that was the only thing that brought them together was sex. This thing with Ralph was quite different than her previous relationship with Jacoby. Months into the relationship Mahogany found out that Ralph slept around with different women in different counties. Mahogany *"Walked through the Valley of the Shadow of Death"* because she could have gotten a Sexual Transmitted disease and it could have been one that took her to her grave. Mahogany could not believe it, she was played by an old cat. Mahogany was not a cheater but she thought that if anyone was going to cheat, it would have been her because of his age and lack of abilities to keep up with their sexual life. Mahogany arrived home from her lonely date night with Ralph. Mahogany tossed and turned in her bed because she needed answers on why he ignored her all night long. Mahogany walked to Ralph's house, knocked on the door until he came to the screen door. "Why are you cheating on me and why did you leave me by myself at the party?" Ralph did not want to talk about why he treated her the way that he did. Ralph stepped outside, grabbed her, through her down and slammed the door in her face. Mahogany knew something was not right with him from the beginning, but she still ignored the warning signs to fill the void. "I should have known better. I have been through this overgrown, still living at home with momma stuff before." Mahogany said to herself. It took Ralph one time to put his hands on her. A light flashed to her past and she took the disappointment with dignity, wiped the dust off of her sandals, walked home without looking back and never spoke to him again. Whatever it was Mahogany had with Ralph was over before it started. Mahogany knew if he put his hands on her one time, he would do it a second time.

After all Mahogany had went through she decided to focus on her career, stay single and practice abstinence. Mahogany found a job working as a Legal Assistant for Jared and Snell Law firm in her hometown. Mahogany loved the fact of being able to help people find justice. Mahogany bank account drastically increased ruling out living paycheck to paycheck. Mahogany saved enough money to trade in her 1992 Dodge Shadow for a midnight green 2000 Toyota Corolla with chrome wheels and tinted windows. Mahogany moved out of her mother's house across town into a big two bedroom, two bath apartment with a fireplace, balcony and washer and dryer connections. Mahogany walked around her apartment proud of how every room she decorated came together in unison representing uniqueness, elegance and luxury living. Mahogany took good care of her son the way she intended. Darrius got everything he needed and wanted. Mahogany shouted with confidence."I have found myself!!!" Moments later Mahogany received a phone for an opportunity of a lifetime. Mahogany was asks to come work for a Real Estate Tax Firm that she applied for in Reo, Texas. They paid twice as much than what she was currently making. Mahogany graciously accepted the offer and put her two weeks notice in at Jared and Snell Law Firm and began working for Trans-Property Real Estate Tax Firm. Mahogany was right where she wanted to be in her life until a distraction came and took her on a detour. Mahogany was informed that her ex-boyfriend Rashad had paroled early and got out of prison. Mahogany was told that Rashad had been asking around town if anyone knew of her whereabouts. Mahogany laid low to avoid running into him at a store or gas station. Hide and Seek came to an end on a Tuesday night when Mahogany heard the door bell ring. Mahogany opened the door and there he was standing in front of her. Mahogany looked him up and down amazed at all of the weight he had lost. Rashad was no longer buff and fluffy. He was just buff. Rashad demeanor had changed. He came with a different talk, heart and mindset. Mahogany was so drawn in by what stood in front of her that she did not reflect on what he had done to her in the past. Mahogany honored the fact that he paid for what he had done. Mahogany reasoned with herself in her thoughts. "Surely by him spending time in prison, it made him reflect on the choices he had made." Mahogany did not want to fight the fact that she was lonely. Mahogany decided to let him pursue her out of loneliness. Mahogany missed having a male companion to whine and dine with. Mahogany ushered him in, offered him refreshments and their conversation took off down memory lane good talking about the good times they shared with each other and his experience in prison. Soon after the conversation dissolved, Mahogany found herself underneath him breaking her dedication to abstinence. Rashad and Mahogany exchanged numbers and saw each other on a regular basis. Rashad was considerate and gentle with her. He catered to her every need. Rashad family and friends invited him and Mahogany out for a couples day out at Chili's. The waiters pushed three tables together and everyone sat, laughed and held off the wall conversations. Mahogany's profession caught the attention of everyone wanting to know more. Mahogany looked over at Rashad and saw that he felt left out. "Rashad, What is the matter?" Mahogany whispered in his ears. Rashad answered her by rolling his eyes at her. The very thing Mahogany thought she was free from came back and slapped her in the face. Mahogany knew it was too good to be true. The evil that was lying dormant in him, stuck it's head up and revealed itself. Mahogany could see the jealousy in Rashad's eyes because the attention was on Mahogany and not on him. "It's not my fault that I am a people's person." "Besides they are your family and friends." Mahogany said within herself. Time was well spent after everybody have eaten, laughed and enjoyed each others company. Everyone said their goodbye's and parted ways. Rashad and Mahogany listened to silence all the way back to Fort Autom. The twenty-five minute drive to Fort Autom seemed like an hour. Mahogany looked out of the window thinking to herself. "How can you turn laughter on and off like that?" Mahogany was happy to see the (Welcome to Fort Autom) city sign. Mahogany asks Rashad if he could swing by her mother's house to pick up Darrius and then drop them off at home. Rashad kept looking forward in silence as if Mahogany did not say a word; but to her surprise he granted her request. Mahogany cradled Darrius in her arms as he slept, buckled him in and got in the car. Rashad drove towards Mahogany's house in silence but his fist spoke loud and clear. Rashad went upside Mahogany's head. Mahogany held the side of her head hoping to bring comfort to the sharp pain that pierced her. Mahogany looked at Rashad and boldly confessed that she had made a mistake given their relationship a second chance; and it would be best if they part ways. Mahogany felt a quick shift that detoured from the direction of her apartment complex. Mahogany have seen Rashad in a rage before, but never have she seen him go completely crazy like this. Mahogany feared for her and her son's life. Rashad eyes were blood shot red with tears rolling down his face, mumbling words to himself that she could not make out. Mahogany mind could not grasp what just happened. Mahogany began questioning herself. What did I do so wrong? What did I do to put him in this state of mind? Why did he wait until we picked up Darrius and decide to go off? The conversation that Rashad had with himself had gotten louder and louder. The demonic spirit of rage had consumed him and made him drive into on coming traffic. Rashad kept driving and Mahogany could see the high beams from a car coming there way. The person driving the car blew their horn and humbly pulled over and waited for him to pass. Rashad turned off onto a dark country road where there was hardly any streetlights. It was pitch dark with nothing but rocky roads and empty fields.

Rashad drove into the deep dark back woods that resembled a scene from a horror movie. Mahogany thought to herself that never in a million years did she think she would encounter a reality scary movie situation. Mahogany mumbled underneath her breath. "Is this really happening?" Mahogany looked back at Darrius and told him that it was going to be alright and they would be home soon. Darrius did not say a word and neither did he shed a tear. Mahogany did not say a word to Rashad because she did not want the state of mind that he was in to get worse. The first thing that came to Mahogany's mind was to pray. Mahogany did not know what to expect going into the deep dark country. Rashad finally spoke. "If I can't have you, then were all going to die." Mahogany looked at Rashad with so much confusion. Rashad looked at Mahogany with so much hatred in his facial expression and told her to shut up. Mahogany did not say another word upon his request. Mahogany began praying to God in silence. She prayed to the one she rejected and turned a def ear to. Mahogany asks God to save them and told Him that if He delivered her and Darrius from *death*, she would never go back to him again. Mahogany pondered on the fact that it was one thing to lose her life because of disobedience, but not the life of her son. Immediately God honored her request. God felt Mahogany's silent tears of fear and heard her humble plea. Mahogany heard something going on with the engine. The car started smoking and making loud noises under the hood as if the engine was getting ready to go out. Rashad snapped out of his demonic trance, grabbed the steering wheel firmly and guided the car off of the road. Rashad was a bit confused because he had just bought the car a couple of days ago. Minutes later after being stranded in the dark country an 18 wheeler passed through on the same dark dirt road that they traveled on. Mahogany knew that if it was not for God's grace and mercy, *death* would have found them in a head on collision. God saved them that night from a near *death* experience. Rashad had been wrestling with the engine for ten minutes shaking wires and cables under the hood, holding a flashlight in his left hand, cursing out every part connected to the engine trying to figure out what went wrong. They saw lights coming up the road, so they stood out to where they would be visible. The gentleman in the truck pulled over and asks Rashad if there's anything he could do. Mahogany knew that God had sent him in their direction. "Yes." Rashad said with relief of finding help. "If you can help me turn this car around somehow and you get behind me and push me across town to my house. I would greatly appreciated." Mahogany stepped away from the light of the truck so the gentleman would not see that she had a knot on her head revealing that they had a fight. Rashad offered to pay him for his trouble. Rashad got in the car and put it in neutral and drove home from a bumper to bumper push all the way across town. Mahogany was grateful that her mother lived two blocks away from Rashad's mother's house. When they arrived, the kind gentleman got out of his truck and ran down a list of things to Rashad about the possibilities of what could be wrong with his car. Mahogany saw a perfect opportunity to grab Darrius and run because their life depended on it. Rashad looked at Mahogany because he saw what she was planning to do. Rashad wanted to stop her by rushing the conversation with the man who generously helped him, but out of respect for what he had done for him, he felt obligated to stand there and listen. Mahogany cradled Darrius in her arms and ran all the way to her mother's house without stopping, just in-case he ran after them. Mahogany ran in her high heel sandals as if she had on athlete tennis shoes. It must have been evident that Mahogany was running for her life because the night walkers shouted at her out of concern. "Are you okay?" Mahogany did not look back nor did she respond. Mahogany ran as if she had seen a ghost. Mahogany made it to her mother's house, turned the key and let herself in huffing and puffing from the run of her life. Shari made sure Mahogany kept a spare key just in-case she needed to come over at anytime. Mahogany walked in the house, put Darrius down and walked to the bedroom that she once slept in and found peace knowing she and Darrius was safe. Shari jumped up out of her bed and saw Mahogany sitting on the bed breathing hard with her head held down. Shari did not asks Mahogany any questions; she just smiled and welcomed her because she knew that her daughter had enough. That was the last time Mahogany had ever spoken or seen Rashad.

## *Self Dialog*

As years went on, I heard of Rashad beating on other women that he dated. I later found out why his behavior was abnormal. He had been dealing with a deep dark issue that he could not talk about to anyone. This is where his anger became so clear to me. He could not go public with being a homosexual because he was afraid of the shame, the torment of being laughed at, judged and criticized. He held the way he really felt on the inside and took it out on women and young children. I found out years later when my son turned fifteen years old that he had gone through the valley of molestation by Rashad at the age of five years old. Rashad is now in prison because my son was not the only victim. There were other little boys who had become victims of his sick perverted behavior. This is not my story to tell. I will let my son testify on this matter when he is ready. When someone is angry for no reason at all. There is a deeper issue lying beneath the surface. Issues come in different packages. Rashad did not look nor act as if he was attracted to men and little boys. It is important to have a close relationship with God. I went through this trial because my relationship with God was at a distance. If I would have stood in my rightful place with God, I would have discerned that spirit early on and saved my son and I pain from mental, physical, sexual, verbal and emotional abuse. No man is worth this kind of trouble. Seek God first before starting a relationship with someone.

The season had changed. Mahogany now at the age of twenty two felt like it was time to experience the party side of life. Mahogany enjoyed the company of her good friend Thomas. They had known each other for years maintaining a friends only relationship. They went out to eat, to the movies and to college football games. The connection between the two was amazing. Thomas knew Mahogany's deepest secrets and she knew his.

Society did not understand how two people of the opposite gender could do everything together and not once take interest in one another. It was Thomas special day and their plans was to bust the club doors wide open. Mahogany made plans to take Thomas to the Kale Harry night club and let him get a couple of drinks on her and cut loose on the dance floor. After all, it was his birthday. Mahogany went all out anticipating what her club experience for the first time will be like. Mahogany went to the mall and picked out an exquisite outfit. Mahogany found herself pleased at the pieces she so carefully put together. Mahogany chose an all black blouse and skirt that fit her curves just right in every way. Mahogany matched her dress to the shoes and accessories that she had already owned. Mahogany had every color shoe and accessory that had ever come out in every style. Mahogany pinned her hair up in a cute pinned up due with curls hanging from both sides of her face while admiring her pedicure and well done acrylic nails. Mahogany knew she was going to look good and nobody could make her think or feel any different. The evening approached and Mahogany was dressed to turn heads. Mahogany modeled amongst herself in the mirror, turning and twisting, admiring everything she put together; even her make up. Her eyeliner was applied just right, the silver eye shadow laid smoothly across her eyelids and the luscious silver lipstick that she coated with gloss made her lips desirable to look upon. Mahogany could not wait to see what Thomas looked like. Thomas and Mahogany always competed with each other to see who would out dress who. Thomas was a sharp well dressed brother that can throw some stuff together that no one would even think of putting together and made look good. The clock struck nine o' clock in the evening and Mahogany turned and twirled in the mirror one last time and headed out of the door. Mahogany drove thirty five mile to Reo to celebrate her best friends special day. Mahogany drove down the highway doing 60 mph singing and hitting whatever note she felt like hitting. "It's your birthday, were gonna party like it's birthday." Mahogany arrived and blew the horn. Thomas looked out of the window signaling that he acknowledge that she was there and that he was coming out. Thomas walked towards the car and

Mahogany opened her mouth because she was somewhat jealous. Mahogany could not deny that Thomas had it going on. The ironic thing was they both had on all black. His hair, mustache and beard was well groomed with no trace of any flaws. The look he had brought out his long eyelashes making Mahogany screen him from head to toe. Thomas had on a black designer shirt with gray and black cuff links, black wide leg slacks that creased down the middle complimenting his body, black and gray Stacey Adam shoes and a Fossil designer watch hanging comfortably from his left wrist. The brother had Mahogany choked up, ready to drink some water. They greeted, complimented each other and hugged. Mahogany thought to herself. "If we were not brothers and sisters......." Mahogany snapped back into reality and allowed Thomas to open up the door for her to get in the car. Kale Harry night club was ten minutes away from Thomas loft. Thomas and Mahogany always looked out for one another. Wherever there was alcohol, they rode together in-case one had a little too much to drink. Thomas and Mahogany arrived at Kale Harry's, paid for valet parking, paid the attendant at the door and went in. They played everything from slow jams, rap, reggae and more. This was a place where grown folks mingled and enjoyed themselves after a hard weeks work. Entering the club was quit an eye catcher. Sitting off to the left was a lounge where couple's set enjoying each others company. On the right was the bar which was filled with people ordering their favorite beverages, laughing and talking. Thomas and Mahogany walked to the lower level and saw a huge dance floor aligned with mirrors surrounding it, reflecting the people dancing and grooving to the beat of the music. To the right was a room where men played pool and arcade games. Thomas and Mahogany ordered a few drinks and headed towards the dance floor. Thomas saw a woman that caught his interest and asks her to dance. Mahogany waived him off and stepped onto the dance floor when she felt a tug asking her to step aside, so he could talk to her away from the all noise. Mahogany looked at the man that tugged on her. Standing before her was a well-dressed light skinned man who's features resembled his youthful teenage years without aging. Mahogany saw him looking at her when she entered the club, but she did not want him to noticed that she noticed him too. "Is that guy your boyfriend?" "Who, Thomas? Goodness no, we are just friends." Mahogany sarcastically said at the nerve of him asking her such a question, as if he was suppose to have already known. "May I have this dance then?" Mahogany led the way to the dance floor moving to the R & B slow jam songs the DJ played to create the atmosphere of love, enticing everyone to feel some type of way. After dancing to a couple of songs Mahogany and her dance partner went to the bar, talked and became acquainted. He introduced himself as Carl. Carl ordered Mahogany's favored drink Crown Royal and coke. He bought as many drinks as she wanted. There conversation was playful and easing until he mentioned that he was ten years older than she was. He's thirty two Mahogany whispered within herself. Carl had a lot going for himself. He had his own home, car and a well paying job. Carl seem to be doing well for himself and likewise, he saw the same in her. The bartender made an announcement. "Last call for alcohol!" Carl and Mahogany exchanged phone numbers hoping the other call first as a genuine sign of interest. Carl and Mahogany connected and spent a lot of time together over the last couple of months and Mahogany decided it was time for Carl to meet Darrius. Carl took to Darrius very well and assured Mahogany that he was well capable of handling the family life. There was never a dull moment with Carl, Darrius and Mahogany. The season changed bringing in the luxury of summer. Shari demanded that Mahogany bring Darrius over for a week to spend time with him. Mahogany packed a couple of Darrius things, dropped him off and hit the highway to meet this man she had become so fond of. Mahogany pulled up and Carl greeted her with hugs and kisses. Carl ordered pizza, popped in a movie, laid a blanket out on the floor as if they were having an indoor picnic. Carl gently brought Mahogany to his chest and locked her comfortably in his arms. Mahogany noticed that Carl brought up the topic of marriage consistently. Carl showed Mahogany in many ways that he was ready to settle down and without a shadow of a doubt; he had found what he had been looking for.

Mahogany brushed him off and did not take his gestures seriously. Mahogany knew that Carl was drawn into to her in such a way that he totally committed all of his free time to her; but not once did she think marriage. The following evening Carl and Mahogany prepared to go out. Carl had a surprise up his sleeve that he was waiting to reveal. Carl took Mahogany to The Lounge Grill & Bar and took the liberty of inviting her friends. Mahogany was lost for words when she saw her friends approach her at the table. It was then Carl got on one knee, spoke to Mahogany in song like words and proposed to her. Carl reminded Mahogany of the love she felt when she dated Jacoby. Mahogany caught her breath from her unexpected surprise and accepted Carl's proposal. Mahogany could not believe it, she was engaged. Mahogany had to admit that she had fallen for him and was not about to let him go. Carl made her feel like no other woman compared to her. Shari and Dorothy Ann loved and treated him as though he was already apart of the family. With all the excitement Mahogany never got a chance to tell her mother that she was engaged. Carl proposed to her on Thursday and informed her that they had an appointment to go before the Judge at the Justice of the Peace to be married. Without consulting Mahogany, Carl went and purchased a marriage certificate a week before he proposed. Carl convinced Mahogany that he could not wait any longer because he had to have her in his life. Mahogany did not have any negative experiences with Carl so she went all the way making their bond official. Mahogany was now a properly married woman. She official carried his last name. Mahogany pondered over the fact that she was now apart of the Zimbabwe African culture. Carl made plans to take Mahogany to Nebraska for their honeymoon to show Mahogany off to his friends. Mahogany never told anyone about the plans Carl planned. Carl informed Mahogany to beware of the Zimbabwe women strife because he did not marry an African woman. All kinds of mix emotions consumed Mahogany. First and far most she got married to quick and now she was in a totally different state and neither family nor friend knew her whereabouts. Carl's male friends welcomed Mahogany and took them to the night club where they played African music all night long. Carl and Mahogany danced until they could not dance anymore. Carl wanted Mahogany to himself away from all of the noise, so Carl asks his friends to take them to a place where romance filled the air. They pulled up in front of a beautiful park next to a beautiful body of water. Carl and Mahogany embraced each and did not let go. They watched the water sparkle from the post lights that made the water shine with such elegance. Art fascinated Mahogany in such a way that she could make the most unattractive thing look beautiful. "Carl, look at the water. A painting of water cannot compare to the real experience of being around water as beautiful as this." Mahogany enjoyed and embraced how beautiful and peaceful it was at the lake. Mahogany poetic words captivated Carl because he grabbed her gently, turned her around and gave her the most heart melting kiss she had ever experienced. Mahogany looked at him with so much passion in her eyes and kissed him again. The heat of the moment came upon them and away they went into the blissful night. The following morning Carl friends cooked breakfast, fixed their plates, served them and they talked, laughed and ate committing the sin of gluttony. Guilty came upon Mahogany as she set stuffing her mouth with bacon and grits. "Oh my God, she still doesn't know." Mahogany took a deep breath and asks her husband for his phone. Mahogany knew that her family had to find out eventually. Mahogany called her mother and son to tell them the good news. Mahogany anticipated on what Shari was going to think, say or do as the phone rung. Shari answered and Mahogany slowly broke down her new life with Carl. Shari kept silent with no interruptions or sign of emotion. Everybody knows that when Shari get silent you better get out of her way. Mahogany finally finished her lengthy explanation about her sudden life changing event when she heard the strangest thing reach her earlobes. Shari out burst of enthusiasm made Mahogany pull the phone away from her ears until she calmed down. "Why you didn't tell me that Carl proposed to you?" Mahogany was a bit shocked that she dodged the dart of fury. "Mom it all happened so fast." Shari spoke to Carl and gave her approval of acceptance into the family. Carl gave Mahogany back the phone relieved that he was officially accepted as son-in-law. Shari expressed her love for Mahogany and excused herself off the phone so she can enjoy her husband. The honeymoon was over and they headed back south to Fort Autom. Carl traveled back and forth from Reo to Fort Autom because his friend had came from Zimbabwe into the United States and lived with him until he found his own place. Carl's friend agreed to split the mortgage but Carl ended up paying his portion month after month. Carl called Mahogany and told her that him and his roommate had a disagreement and he could no longer take care of a grown man. Mahogany felt his pain because she knew how he leached off of his generosity. Mahogany thought long and hard about the situation and came up with a second option. Mahogany ask Carl if he wanted to move in with her and Darrius to get rid of his roommate. Carl was a provider and that was one of the things she loved about him. He was not about to move in with his wife. He wanted to lead by example. Carl went and spoke to his boss about living on sight on a property where he worked. Carl maintained the up keeping of a small community of two story brick homes. Carl's boss agreed and her and Darrius moved to Reo, Texas. They were now a residence of Palm County. The house that Carl had gotten was a mystery to Mahogany because she had not yet seen it. Mahogany trusted Carl's judgment. Upon arrival, Mahogany noticed that the house that his boss put him in was small and nowhere big enough for a family of three. Mahogany great expectations shattered when she saw the place they called home. Mahogany had hopes of her husband getting into one of the two story houses that he managed. Carl settled for a house fit for a bachelor. Mahogany walked in the house and felt like she was in an efficiency apartment. Mahogany thought to herself. "I moved from a nice size apartment to a matchbox." Mahogany stopped herself from complaining and acknowledged the fact that she was a married woman now and it was only fair to make the best of it since the move was sudden. Mahogany knew with the mindset her husband had, he would find a bigger place for his family in no time. Mahogany wanted to please her husband in every way. Mahogany took interest in studying the Zimbabwe language and foods. Mahogany heard a bunch of laughing and a language she did not understand. Carl's friends whom Mahogany had never seen before pulled up by the dozens in front of the house. Mahogany had never experienced anything like this before. Without informing Carl that they were coming. They pulled up in herds, walked into the house and went straight to the refrigerator. Mahogany thought she was having an illusion when she saw them gathered at her refrigerator getting full off of their food and beer. Mahogany tilted her head to the side, folded her arms and looked at her rude, disrespectful, unwanted guest, bomb rushing their refrigerator. Mahogany did not play about her house. One of Mahogany's biggest pet peeves was house traffic. Mahogany despised house traffic especially after a good sweeping and mopping. Popping up at their house unannounced became a consistent thorn and got on Mahogany's last nerves. It wasn't enough that they were disrespectful and inconsiderate. They took the initiative upon themselves to pop up even while Carl was a work. Carl worked on the property but that did not give his friends the right to have access to their home. Mahogany found out that her husband had given them permission to come over whenever they wanted without consulting her. Mahogany went from chile mode to boiling within seconds. "How could he be so selfish and self centered to not include me in making a decision that was so important?" "Did he forget that he was no longer a single man?" "I got a remedy for that." The following morning Mahogany locked both locks to the front door as soon as Carl left for work to keep the leaches from entering. Mahogany left the back door unlocked just in case Carl came home in-between work orders. Mahogany finally had time alone to enjoy herself. Mahogany pinned her hair up in a clip, filled the tub up with milk and honey bubble bath and laid back in the tub allowing her body to relax. Mahogany enjoyed the serenity around her until she heard footsteps going through the house. Mahogany thought that Carl had come home on his break to relax a little. "Carl honey. What do you want for dinner tonight?" Mahogany waited for a response but instead she got silence. "Maybe he didn't hear me." Mahogany gave it everything she had reaching the highest note that she was capable of. "CARL. WHAT DO YOU WANT FOR DINNER TONIGHT." Mahogany gave it all that she had again, but still there was nothing. "CARL. WHY ARE YOU NOT ANSWERING ME?" Mahogany thought that was the strangest thing because he unusually responds to her. Mahogany stepped out of her imagination of a spa, put on her robe, walk in the living-room and found out that Carl was not in the house at all. One of Carl's friends had let himself in through the back door when he discovered that he did not have access to the front door. "What are you doing here!!!!!" Carl heard Mahogany screaming from one of the nearby properties he was working on and ran as fast as he could, dropping every tool he had in his hand. Carl came in and Mahogany took the heat off of his friend and turned it towards her husband. Mahogany told him that his friend scared the mess out of her and that it was all his fault because he gave them permission to come and go as they pleased. Mahogany confronted Carl on the matter because she was tired of being silent and nice. Mahogany explained to Carl that she was in the tub and thought she was talking to him. "Carl, your friend did not even respond. He kept silence and led me on to believe that you was just ignoring me." "Do he not have a mouth to speak?" "Carl, I was frighten when I got out of the tub and found him sitting in our living-room." "Carl, your friends cannot keep coming over here when they get ready." The disapproving look on Carl's face when Mahogany mentioned change. Carl attitude changed and began running down his customs to her. Carl explained to Mahogany that back home in Africa they do not call or give early notice of visitation; they just show up. "Carl, you are a married man now and some of the things that you use to do while single, you can no longer do those things because you have a family to consider." Carl confronted Mahogany and Mahogany did not say a word until he finished. Mahogany spoke up because she clearly saw where the conversation was headed, and it was not towards peace and understanding. Mahogany broke it down to Carl in terms that he can understand because clearly what she said before was not sinking in at all. "Carl you should be considerate of my custom as well and we call before visiting." Carl must have forgotten that Mahogany had been studying his customs and nowhere did she read that in Africa they come and go in and out of people's houses as they please. Mahogany looked at Carl hoping that he would grasps the words coming out of her mouth. Mahogany tried to bring awareness to Carl that she was trying and that he needed to come into realization that he married and American woman and not an African woman. Mahogany let Carl know that it was unfair to her for him to throw his customs on her all at once. Mahogany reminded Carl that when they were dating, she never encountered such disrespect coming from him. "If I had known then what I know now, things would have been a little different. "KNOW YOUR PLACE MAHOGANY!" "I AM THE ONE PAYING ALL OF THE BILLS AND YOU HAVE NO SAY SO IN THE DECISION MAKING CONCERNING MY FRIENDS!" Mahogany looked at Carl with a devastating look on her face because her husband has never talked to her like that before. Rage rose up in Mahogany. "Look Carl, you told me that you did not want me to work because you believe in taken care of your family." Mahogany reassured that she was not going to be a slave to his customs. She was not having it, especially in her own house. The peace and strong bond they once shared no longer rested within their marriage. Carl was no longer a husband or a friend. He became a stranger and an enemy. Carl became very bitter and stubborn towards Mahogany in order to prove a point to his friends that he was the head of the household. Carl wanted to please his friends in order to keep them in his life. Carl's friends knew how to take advantage of him because of his soft heart and lack of courage to say; "No." His friends knew that if they wanted to have a good time, all they had to do was connect with Carl. Carl was their supply house. His motto to them was (Whatever you need, when you need it. Just know, I got it)." Carl supplied all of the beer, food and on a lot of occasions money. Mahogany could not understand for the life of her, why they did not want to stay home with their own wives. Mahogany concluded after studying Carl's friends behavior they were jealous of their marriage. They were jealous of how Carl adored Mahogany. Carl's friends knew that milking him out of money, beer and food had to come to a halt because of marriage. Mahogany did not believe in separating or stopping Carl from mingling with his friends. That would be selfish. Mahogany just wanted Carl to understand that there has to be balance between family and friends. Memorial Day came and Carl and Mahogany put together a gathering for family and friends to come and feast. Shari and Dorothy Ann came up for the holidays and helped Mahogany prepare a buffet of African and American food. Carl and Mahogany hosted their first annual Memorial Day celebration dinner. It seemed as if everyone from Zimbabwe was there. Shari, Dorothy Ann and Mahogany went out with style for the dinner party. The backyard was decorated in red, white and blue party favors and the food set on a long rectangular table covered by an elegant table cloth. People covered the backyard as if they were attending a concert. The music filled the air and the people danced and chatted, having themselves a good old time. Carl's friends brought their wives and Mahogany had the pleasure of meeting them for the first time. Mahogany could tell by the way they looked at each other that they did not like her. Carl warned her about how the Zimbabwe women felt about African men marrying American women. The Zimbabwe women greeted her with their fake smiles and hand shakes, excluding her out of their conversation by speaking in their language with no intent on translating. Mahogany was not fluent enough in the language to quit understand, so she felt alone. What seemed like five hours was just only one hour. Two women pulled up in the driveway without the company of a man. They were fairly nice looking women that looked more American than they did African. The wives of Carl's friends invited them over to be apart of the celebration. They got out of the van greeted their friends with a hug and immediately they took both of their friends over to Carl and introduced them to him. Mahogany could see the evil plot in their hearts a mile away. Mahogany knew that they were out to tempt her husband. Mahogany put her drink down, walked over to where her husband was and stood her ground. Mahogany walked up to the women letting them know that she was the woman of the house. Mahogany interrupted their conversation and introduced herself. Mahogany gave them a proper welcome and thanked them for being apart of her and her husbands first celebration dinner. Mahogany lied, knowing that she did not want them there and she wished they would go home. Mahogany dreaded them coming over because she knew who they were after. Mahogany walked off and attended to her mother and grandmother. Time drew near and Mahogany's mother and Dorothy Ann, packed up and headed home exhausted from feeding what seem like all of Africa. Darrius went to his room to play with his remote control car that Shari had bought him. Mahogany noticed that everyone was leaving. Mahogany looked around for Carl until she saw him standing on the drivers side of the van with a piece of paper and pin in his hands. Mahogany stood there looking directly at her husband entertaining this woman who was new to the United States. Carl friend's and their wives found it amusing that James took interest in this other woman. Mahogany could see the smirch on their faces. The Zimbabwe women looked over and saw Mahogany looking at the connection being made between Carl and the lady they invited. They were on a mission and accomplished it without any effort. Carl and Mahogany found themselves alone with each other cleaning up the mess that scattered over the back yard in silence. Mahogany wanted to get to the bottom of things, but she did not want to confront him in front of company, so she waited until the opportune time. Mahogany finally broke the silence. "What was that all about?" Carl looked into Mahogany's eyes and informed her that if anyone comes over from Zimbabwe, Africa and they reside in the same city, they exchange contact info and stay in contact with one another. Mahogany understood and left it alone. What was innocent mingling for him was not innocent mingling on his friends behalf. August approached and Mahogany enrolled Darrius at Reo Rock Elementary. Darrius was excited about being around other children his age. Mahogany made up in her mind that she was going to find a job while Darrius was at school. Inspite of what her husband wishes were; she was not compromising, after all, he did not compromise with her. Mahogany lowered her standards in the job market quite a bit. Mahogany began working for Reo Airline Call Center working five days a week from the hours of 11 pm to 7 am. Mahogany work schedule was bitter sweet because she could get Darrius to school by 7:45am and be there to pick him up at 4pm and Carl was there to watch him through the night. James saw this as an opportunity to entertain his friends by offering their house as a place to relax, eat and drink without Mahogany around to say a word. Mahogany expected to come from work to prepare Darrius for school, take a bath, put on her pajamas and sleep. Mahogany took Darrius to school but finding relaxation was at a distance because Carl and his friends mingled and made a mess of the house and expected Mahogany to clean it up. Friday had come and Mahogany prepared Darrius luggage to spent the weekend with his cousin Shelton. Mahogany had to work over the weekend so that worked out perfectly for her. Mahogany went to work that night and enjoyed the fact that the work was very slow. About 1:00 am the computers shut down. The IT department could not get their fingers on what caused the computers to shut down. Mahogany and her co-workers eased through the first couple of hours until the supervisor made the announcement for everyone to go home. Mahogany was excited because she had a chance to go home and go to sleep beside her husband. Mahogany clocked out, got in her car, sped out of the parking lot and merged onto highway 85. Mahogany made it home about 3:00 am. Mahogany pulled up and saw a little red car in the driveway parked behind Carl's car. Mahogany's first thought was that he went to an auction and bought another car. Buying cars and fixing them up was a hobby to bring in extra income. Mahogany parked by the curb in front of the house. Mahogany stuck her key in the lock but to her surprise, both locks were locked. Mahogany concluded that he was probably tired and it was all just an innocent mistake. Mahogany blew it off and did not think anything of it. Mahogany opened the gate to the backyard and entered the house through the back door. Mahogany walked a couple of steps down which was suppose to be somewhat of a hallway, stopped, took off her heels and rubbed her feet. Mahogany entered her pitch dark bedroom, flipped on the light switch and saw Carl, her husband in the bed with another woman sleep in his arms. Carl committed adultery on her. Carl was too deep in his sleep to even notice that Mahogany was in the room. At that moment, another side of Mahogany came out that she did not know was there. Mahogany acted out in such a way that his mistress did not know whether to run or stay hid behind Carl. Carl jumped up in shock of seeing his wife home early. Carl could not find the words to say because he knew he had been caught in adultery. Carl knew he had messed up. "Girl, put your clothes on, get out of my bed and get out of my house!" Mahogany did not go after the woman, she turned her fury towards her husband because he knew better. He stood their and made vows before her and God. Mahogany did not leave any room for explanations. Seeing him in the act was explanation enough. "Carl you cheated on me." Carl must have been drunk because his response was the wrong answer. Carl looked at his wife with a straight face. "Why not?" Mahogany looked at Carl, put her hands on her hips, turned her head to the side and took anger to another level. Mahogany did not care what was of value in that house, all she could think about was retaliation. Mahogany made her statement and when she was done, the house looked like a bulldozer had hit it. Carl had gotten real angry. Carl did not get angry because Mahogany had tore up their house. He was angry because his sin was exposed. Carl put his clothes on and went to the shed where he kept his tools. Carl grabbed a thick iron pipe and struck Mahogany with it as if she was a burglar who had trespassed by breaking and entering. Carl drug Mahogany out of the house unto the pavement striking her again with the iron pipe. Carl mistress saw that as an opportunity to get in her car and go. Mahogany reached in her pocket, grabbed her cell phone and dialed 911. The police came and called for an ambulance to check out Mahogany. One of the officers took pictures of Mahogany's face while the other banged on the door calling for Carl to come out. Carl opened the door and the police read him his rights, put him in handcuffs and placed him in the backseat of the police car. The police asks who messed up the house and Mahogany confessed. The police asks Carl why did he hit her. Carl stated he was trying to protect himself. Mahogany shouted at the police. "Officer, I HAD A RIGHT TO GET UPSET. HE

HAD ANOTHER WOMAN IN OUR BED." Carl mumbled something under his breath. "What did you say Carl? I can go for round two." The officer calmed Mahogany down, told her to go in the house because her husband was going to jail."That serves him right." Mahogany said. The weekend had past and Mahogany had the house looking as if nothing destructive had happened. Carl posted bail, called Mahogany and told her to come pick him up. Mahogany looked at the phone and told her cheating husband to call the woman that he cheated with to pick him up. Carl walked all the way from the county jail to Mills Creek blvd. Carl came in and told Mahogany either she was going to move out voluntarily or he was going to move somewhere else forcing her to move. The next day Mahogany found an apartment up north, paid the deposit and got the approval to move in at the end of the week. The end of the week had come. Mahogany rented a U-Haul and started moving her stuff with the help of family and friends. Mahogany told Carl that she would be out by the end of the week. Carl shook his head in agreement and continued on in silence towards her. Mahogany went back and forth loading up the truck when the phone rang. Mahogany answered the phone and was met with pure silence. "Hello." "Hi, is Carl there?" "No he's not." "I am Carl's wife what business do you have with Carl?" "We are seeing each other." The lady became furious because she did not even know that Carl was married. In speaking with the woman on the phone Mahogany found out that she was not the woman that she caught in her bed. Carl had been cheating on her the entire four months of their marriage. Mahogany hung up the phone and sped up the moving process. Mahogany went into the closet to gather her clothes when she saw that Carl's safe was not completely closed. Mahogany knew that Carl had to have left his safe open on accident because he kept it locked at all times. Mahogany bent down to look in and found four empty boxes and one full box of condoms. Behind the boxes, Mahogany found love letters and thinking of you cards. Mahogany knew at that point there was no chance of future reconciliation. Mahogany collected the evidence to use against him in divorce court; and as promised, her and Darrius moved out of the house they once called home. The living room furniture, bedroom furniture and everything in the kitchen and bathroom belonged to Mahogany. Mahogany looked around the matchbox that her husband, Darrius and her had once shared, closed the door, locked it and put the spare key under the door mat and did not look back. The only thing that was left in the house was Carl's shoes and clothes. Shari taught Mahogany and Sharron well. Shari taught them to never go into a marriage with nothing; always go with something. Mahogany loved the thought of no longer having to deal with a cheating husband and neither did she have to put up with his friends and their customs. Mahogany thought that what she had with Carl was true love; until she realized that if it was true love, it would not have slapped her in the face. Mahogany looked around her new apartment but she was not completely satisfied. Mahogany stood in the middle of her barely used living room and began thinking about the countless women who probably have set on her couch while she was at work. Mahogany pondered on the countless women that Carl had in her bed infesting it with adultery. Anger rose up in Mahogany and she decided to throw every piece of furniture away from the living room to the bedroom. Afterward Mahogany felt good and her spirit at piece. Mahogany and Darrius set and slept on the floor for weeks. Mahogany wanted to start over by getting new furniture. Time went on and Mahogany lost her job do the economy. Mahogany received a letter of eviction giving her three days to evacuate the premises. Mahogany called a married couple that she met through Carl from Zimbabwe. Mahogany told them that her and Carl's marriage had ended and about her unemployment situation. They never came around because they did not approve of Carl's behavior. No matter the occasion, they did not participate. They put in a good word for Mahogany at their apartment complex and the manager approved Mahogany's application and within two days Mahogany and Darrius had a new home.

Mahogany enrolled Darrius in the Tidale Independent School District. Mahogany found another job working for the government at a company called the US Currency as a customer service representative. Mahogany worked Monday-Friday and had weekends off to spend time with Darrius. All of Mahogany's bills was paid with one check and did whatever she wanted to do with the second check. Darrius enjoyed going to the YMCA after school program and Mahogany started a dance ministry at her father's church. Mahogany was living the high life until the season changed. Mahogany drove down the highway singing and banging the palm of her hand on the steering wheel jamming to the group Earth, Wind and Fire. Mahogany was tuned into her own little world when a gentleman honked his horn pointing down at her left front tire. "Oh crap, what is wrong with my tire." Mahogany waved her hand as a sign of thank you. Mahogany took the next exit, turned into the Race Track gas station to put some air in her tire. Mahogany looked through her side mirror and saw the guy that flagged her down pull up behind her at the gas station. He got out, walked to her car and looked at her tire. Mahogany was struck with how gorgeous he was. He introduced himself as Keon. Keon offered his assistance and struck a conversation with Mahogany. The things that came out of his mouth sent flash signals of warning. Mahogany chose to ignore them because she was tired of being alone. Mahogany had been alone for awhile and she wanted to put an end to her drought. Mahogany had no social life. Mahogany went to work, church and back home. Mahogany found out that Keon lived in the city of Millshire with his mother. Mahogany swallowed deeply when he announced where he lived. Mahogany heard about the community he lived in on the news and by word of mouth through people that were familiar with the neighborhood. Murders were committed and prostitute polluted the neighbor and the drug infestation overwhelmed it. Mahogany did not want any part of that, so she stayed away. Keon convinced Mahogany that it was unfair to judge a neighborhood based on other people's bad choices. Besides, what was going on in his neighborhood had nothing to do with him, he just live there. Mahogany swallowed her fear of Millshire and paid him a visit. After spending some time with Keon in Millshire Mahogany found out that Millshire was not as bad as people made it out to be. Keon and his family welcomed Mahogany and Darrius as if they were apart of the family. Mahogany loved the fact that they were family oriented. Everything they did, they did it together. Keon family always gathered together whether it was for a football game, Sunday dinner or whether they just wanted to kick it, drink or play dominoes. Keon parents spoiled Darrius and treated him as though he was their biological grandchild. Things became serious between Keon and Mahogany and what was a household of two had become a household of three. Things were great and Mahogany had gotten another job offer at International Mortgage. Mahogany took the offer making more money than she'd ever had before. Everything was going smooth until she hit a bump in the road. Mahogany was back to step 1. She found herself shacking and fornicating again. Four months into the relationship, Mahogany found out that there was going to be an added addition to the family. Mahogany was bringing another child into this world out of wedlock. Mahogany traded her 2000 Toyota Corolla in for a red 2002 Mitsubishi Lancer. Shortly after the purchase of the new car, Keon asks Mahogany if he could keep the car to look for a job. The fact that he wanted to look for a job to provide for his family made her blush. Keon dropped Mahogany off at work every morning at 7:30 am. Mahogany wanted to believe the word he spoke to her were true. Mahogany looked out of the window from her upstairs apartment and saw that a couple was moving into the building across from them who happen to live together as common law married. It's something about their presence that changed the atmosphere for the worst. What was once peaceful became seriously disturbed. The neighbor across the way continually cheated and beat his girlfriend, time, after time, after time again. Mahogany felt her pain. She knew it all too well. She could relate to living in fear and being a slave in her own house. Keon became acquainted with the neighbor across the way allowing him to have a major influence on his life. Keon set with him and told him that it was not cool for a man to beat on a woman. The neighbor interrupted Keon in the midst of his conversation and told him that he had to beat her, because that was the only way to get her to do what he demanded. The sun set and the cool of the night consumed the earth. Keon came in the house intoxicated demanding Mahogany give him sex. Mahogany declined. Keon put his demand on Mahogany for the second time and once again she declined. Keon went into an outraged because that spirit that was operating in him did not like rejection. Keon took his fist and beat Mahogany as though she did not carry his child. Once again Mahogany found her self a victim of physical abuse. Mahogany once again found herself *"Walking through the Valley of the Shadow of Death."* Mahogany past flashed before her eyes. Mahogany remembered the pain she suffered and refuse to let another man ruin her life. Mahogany bawled up her fist and fought back with all of her strength. On that day Keon found out that Mahogany was a little on the crazy side and left her alone. The following morning Keon woke up feeling the effects from Mahogany's hard blows with her fist. "Ouch...man....." Keon came into the bedroom showing Mahogany how much damage she had done to his face. Mahogany looked at him, turned over and focus on the movie on television. Keon went outside and set with the neighbor from across the way. Mahogany over heard their neighbor pumping Keon head up with negative advice on how to deal with a woman. He told Keon that he will never let a woman do him this way Mahogany did him last night. Did he not know that it was his advice that influenced Keon to provoke her? Keon indulged himself to another day of binge drinking. Keon came into the house drunk demanding Mahogany to give him sex. Mahogany was seven months pregnant and her belly showed ever bit of it. Keon knew Mahogany could not move around all that well, so he used it to his advantage. Keon took his neighbors advise and beat her until Mahogany gave into his demands. Mahogany laid there aching with pain, while her boyfriend claimed victory from her submission. Mahogany woke up sore from the physical abuse she encountered the night before. Calling in absent was not a choice for Mahogany. She had to go to work to make sure all of the bills and necessities of the house was met. Keon convinced himself that he could get an allowance out of Mahogany's check because he could not find a job. Mahogany had enough of Keon's non-sense. Mahogany gave Keon two options. Either he was going to leave her house immediately or keep looking for another job. Mahogany saw the opportunity to have a heart to heart conversation with Keon regarding the neighbor across the way. Mahogany assured him that if he keep going in the path which his so called friend is telling him to travel he is going to run into trouble and it's going to be more than what he bargained for. Keon blocked out everything Mahogany told him and allowed every word to travel through one ear and out of the other. Mahogany went to bed in peace knowing that she released how she felt inside. Mahogany woke up for work rejuvenated and feeling good about going to work. Mahogany arrived and discovered that International Mortgage decided to downsize because the economy had gone down and no one wanted to purchase a home. Mahogany was amongst the seven that had been elected to leave. Mahogany figured that they did not want to pay her while she was on maternity leave. Mahogany took it all in but what she dreaded the most was having to break down the awful news about losing her job to Keon. Keon pulled up with the music on full blast doing an off beat dance and singing off tune. Keon told Mahogany the good news about finally getting a job. Mahogany took a deep breath relieved that Keon's good news made it that much easier to tell him that she had lost her job. Mahogany proceeded in telling Keon the news and he reassured her that she did not have to worry about a thing because he had everything under control. Keon was offered a maintenance position working for an apartment complex across town. Keon attitude changed for the better. Keon was happier than he had ever been. Mahogany relaxed in the shower when she found out the water from the shower was not the only water running down her legs. "KEON, MY WATER BROKE!" Mahogany went in labor for seven hours and on January 15, 2004 Tyler made his entrance into the world. Keon took hold of his first born and promised to take care of his family. Keon did as promised until things took a turn for the worse. Keon's job was short lived. Keon could not handle the pressure of being an unemployed man that was not able to take care of his family. Keon became unstable mentally and emotionally, so he returned back to his bad habits. Mahogany experienced this once too many times in her previous relationships Mahogany could not take anymore of his bullying. Besides, she have two children to consider. Darrius and Tyler should not have to bare pain because of the poor choices that their mother had made. Keon hung out with the neighbor all night smoking and indulging in alcohol. Keon staggered in the house drunk demanding sex from Mahogany. Mahogany declined and this time she was going to stand her ground. Keon hit Mahogany with his right fist and then his left. The pain from the hit stung Mahogany and made her ball up and cry. Mahogany sucked up her tears and told Keon to run for his life. Keon stood solid and did not take Mahogany seriously. Mahogany got up from the floor, took anger to another level and chased him out of her house until he ran across the street. Somebody must have felt sorry for him because he managed to scrap up some change and called Mahogany from a pay phone. Keon begged and pleaded with Mahogany to let him come back home. Mahogany stood her ground and told him that what he suggested was impossible and what they had was over. Mahogany had been through enough in her life with guys that felt that beating a woman made them a man. "Mahogany can I just come in and get my clothes?" Keon pleaded. Mahogany took the phone away from her ear and looked at it. "No, if you want your clothes you can pick them up outside in a trash bag at the end of the stairs and then she hung up. Mahogany went to her room, packed up the few clothes he had and from that point on, Mahogany had no other dealing with him outside of their son's affairs.

# CHAPTER TWELVE

## *The Valley of Struggles*

## *(Single Parenting)*

### *Self Dialog*

I am blessed to parent two of the greatest sons on earth. They have constantly put a smile on my face. They have encouraged and shown me how to love and what it feels like to be loved. No matter the struggles we faced, they did not complain. My two sons understood we were going to be alright even though we walked through the valley of struggles. I became a mother at the age of 14 years old. When I look back over all my life all I can say is "Thank you Lord." I could not have managed any of this without God. God had to purge me in order to impart into me. God had to shake me and put me in uncomfortable places in order for me to stand solid in Him and Him only. It is not easy being single and raising children. Yes, it gets frustrating, it gets hard at times and it can seem like a ware and tare. The beauty of it all is that children are gifts from God. This gives us the opportunity to love them, nurture them, teach them, guide them and release them for purpose. We are blessed to have each other through the low times and through the high times. We know each others strengths and we know each other weaknesses. We are gifts from God to one another. I could not have survived without them and they have told me, that they could not have survived without me. I told my sons when they were little even until now that they are handsome, they are hearers and doers of Gods word, they will be successful, a great husband and father to their children. I speak over my children. The devil is constantly speaking and that's why we have to intervene and speak over them who God says they are. I teach my children to look past what's popular and do what is right in the eyes of God. I am blessed to have sons that is young in age but mature in spirit. Their character resembles that of an elderly man with great wisdom, knowledge and understanding. They are very smart and God has called them to preach His word. Life as a single mother has it's reward and it's challenges. The key is staying focused on the Messiah. The one who reigns over ever circumstance, no matter the trial. I never had regrets about having my children. I do admit that my boys with the help of God settle me down from my worldly ways. I have raised my sons alone, even though they know their father. God taught me how to love, nurture and provide for my children spiritually and emotionally, I had to learn how to take on a double dose of responsibilities. I had to learn that it was no longer about me because I have two sons that needed me more than anything. My children needed my love and my support in the home and in extra curricular activities. Single parenting takes a lot of fasting, praying, strength, endurance, patients, love and structure.

## Spiritual Food for Thought

**Proverbs 22:6** *states: Train up a child in the way he should go: and when he is old, he will not depart from it.*

# Self Dialog

As a young single parent I taught my children and my children taught me. They taught me what it was like to build a relationship. They taught me what it was like to sacrifice. They taught me how to juggle many task at one time. They have taught me how to stand, even when I did not feel like standing. While they were teaching me, I became more educated and rooted in what it took to be a mother. I must say it is not easy because there are many times that you wish the father or if your a single man raising kids the mother was there to step in and ease some of the load. In my case I had to teach my sons how to love a woman for who she is and not for what she has. As a single parent I had to have survival skills and be the hero. You have to smile even when you do not feel like smiling. You have to push when you do not feel like pushing. You have to do this to let your children know that quitting is not an option. It is not always peaches and cream because there will be misunderstandings. As a single parent there were times I locked myself up in my room and cried. As a single parent most of the times things are good and sometimes it seems as if the weight of the world dropped in on me. There were times the money was scares and I could not get the clothes they needed. I know what it feels like to send the children to school with only two to three new shirts and pants. There were times that I did not know where the next meal was going to come from. There were times we had nothing to eat but ketchup sandwiches, mayonnaise sandwiches, syrup sandwiches, peanut butter and jelly sandwiches. There were plenty of nights our meal consist of rice and can goods. I know what it was like to depend on government assistance to pay my bills. I know what it feels like to go to different food pantries to feed my children. There were days I had to depend on family to bring what they had out of their refrigerator just to make sure my kids and I had something to eat. I know the struggle and worry of facing eviction because I could not afford to pay the rent. I know the struggle of having to sit in a dark house with candles lit because I could not pay the light bill. I know what it is like to depend on city transportation.

I know the struggle of having to dress the children and walk everywhere you want to go near and far in good and bad weather. I know the struggle of having a hotel address as my kids and I place of residence. I know what it is like to have to come out of my comfort zone. I know what it's like to have to spend days and weeks in the hospital with my son because of heart issues and earring loss in both of his ears. I know what it is like to get fired from jobs because I had to miss work and attend to my child's health issues. I know what it's like to knock the wind out of a child because of teenage mood swings. Yes, we had our good moments and bad moments. The thing I loved is that no matter what we went through we did not dwell on what was going on with and around us because we walked by faith and not by sight. Yes, we had struggles but inspite of what we went through we stayed positive. We knew where our help came from. We knew who our provider and doctor was (Jesus). Inspite of the storms or afflictions we went about our business everyday saying it could have been worse. I bless God that they were able to live at home and did not have to live permanently in a hospital. We understood that God was bigger than anything that we had ever been through. We could have been on the streets but God was a constant shelter. We could have moved into the hospital room never seeing the inside of a home again but God has been our constant doctor. We could have been without clothes and something to eat but God was our constant provider. God was there all the time. God has never left us nor did He ever forsake us.

## Spiritual Food for Thought

*Matthew 6:25-35 states: 25. Therefore I say unto you, Take no thought for your life, what ye shall eat, or what ye shall drink; nor yet for your body, what ye shall put on. Is not the life more than meat, and the body than raiment? 26. Behold the fowls of the air: for they sow not, neither do they reap, nor gather into barns; yet your heavenly Father feedeth them. Are ye not much better than they? 27. Which of you by taking thought can add one cubit unto his stature? 28. And why take ye thought for raiment? Consider the lilies of the field, how they grow; they toil not, neither do they spin; 29. And yet I say unto you, That even Solomon in all his glory was not arrayed like one of these. 30 Wherefore, if God so clothe the grass of the field, which to day is, and to morrow is cast into the oven, shall he not much more clothe you, O ye of little faith? 31. Therefore take no thought, saying, What shall we eat? or, What shall we drink? or, Wherewithal shall we be clothed? 32. (For after all these things do the Gentiles seek:) for your heavenly Father knoweth that ye have need of all these things. 33. But seek ye first the kingdom of God, and his righteousness; and all these things shall be added unto you. 34. Take therefore no thought for the morrow: for the morrow shall take thought for the things of itself. Sufficient unto the day is the evil thereof.*

## Spiritual Food for Thought

*2 Timothy 3:16-17 states:* [16] *All scriptures is given by inspiration of God, and is profitable for doctrine, for reproof, for correction, for instruction in righteousness:* [17] *That the man of God may be perfect, thoroughly furnished unto all good works.*

## Self Dialog

Single parenting is what you make it. As a parent, I have taught, rebuked and rewarded my children. Sometimes when we rebuke our children, it hurts, but it's necessary. I love my children too much to let them say and do whatever they feel. If a parent love their children, they will stand their ground and stand firm to rules and guidelines that will build and make them strong.

Believe it or not, children they will respect you when they know that you care. Many children go astray because the parent/s want to be their child's friend, instead of their parent. We are in the end times where children are telling their parents what they are going to do and what they are not going to do. This generation do not have respect for their elders. This generation of children are rolling their eyes, snapping their fingers, rolling their necks, fighting, stealing and cursing out their parents. I don't know about your house but I refuse to let the child I brought in this world disrespect me. These children are our responsibility and it starts at home. If you love your child you will teach the ways of the Lord. The Lord loves us so much that he shows us tough love. We should want our children to avoid the same mistakes that we made growing up. Don't get me wrong our children are going to make mistakes but it should not be the mistake that could have been avoided, if we had done our job as parents. If we don't get involved with our children the juvenile jail, the prison system or an early grave will. I had to change my way of doing things so my children would not find love in the streets. As parents we will make mistakes but it should not be the same mistake over and over again. How many parents had to stand over their child's casket because the child wanted to fill their void in the ways of the world? I know it's a struggle but it is better to correct them in love according to the word of God because if not, the blood will be on your hands. Listen when I say this. Do not beat on your children just to be beating on them. No child deserves abuse. Never whip your child when your really angry. The bible speaks about how parents should not provoke their children. The same way you reward them out of love, you deal with them in correction out of love. Your children will respect and appreciate you more when you show them that your doing it all for their well being. My boys may not understand or like everything that I do, but they will see the results as they live. If it's the Lords will, they will come back and thank me, for I will not lose my children to the wickedness of this world. I will not allow satan to do whatever he wants with them on earth just to take them to his camp called (Hell) and burn them in the lake of fire, garnish their teeth and make mockery out of them for eternity. The struggle is real but it can be done. Don't give up your child to this world without a fight. My boys are my gift from God and He entrusted me with their life.

## *Spiritual Food for Thought*

**Proverbs 13:24** *states: 24. He that spareth his rod hateth his son: but he that loveth him chasteneth him betimes.*

## *Spiritual Food for Thought*

**Proverbs 23:13-14** *states: 13. Withhold not correction from a child: for if thou strike him with the rod, he shall not die. 14. Thou shalt beat him with the rod, and deliver his soul from hell.*

## *Spiritual Food for Thought*

**Ephesians 6:4** *states: 4. And, ye fathers, provoke not your children to wrath: but bring them up in the nurture and admonition of the Lord.*

## *Spiritual Food for Thought*

**Isaiah 41:10** *states: 10. "So do not fear, for I am with you; do not be dismayed, for I am your God. I will strengthen you and help you; I will uphold you with my righteous right hand."*

# Self Dialog

In this journey called (parenting) I have learned to reward them when it is time to be rewarded and correct them when correction is needed. I have had my share of adventures just by being in their presence. They have given me life, just as much as I have given them life. What we have been through good and bad did not kill us, it just built us up and brought us closer together as a family. We value one another and we do not take it lightly. I have learned from seeing other parents and their children. With the help of God, take the time out to teach your kids about the Word of God (Bible). This is something that we as parents cannot do ourselves. It takes the Father above all to bring us through second by second, minute by minute, hour by hour, day by day, month by month and year by year. Be patient, be understanding, be willing to endure at all cost. Do not let the world raise and teach your children for you. Our children need us to stand on our post for them through the good, the bad, the ugly and the greater. Weathering the storm with my boys has made our bond as mother and son stronger than before. Our kids watch every thing we do. This is why we have to be careful because they mirror our behavior.

# CHAPTER THIRTEEN

## *The Valley of Being Pimped and Prostituted by Leaders and Church Folks*

### *Self Dialog*

**The definition or theory of abuse:**

*It is the improper usage or treatment of an entity, often to unfairly or improperly gain benefit.*

In the world of spiritual abuse there are some leaders and church folks who are out to solicit themselves as the one who will teach you, lead you and help push you to purpose but they come by way of an unclean spirit to deprive people of their gifts and anointing. The leaders and church folks that are doing this for their own personal gain. It's about what a person can contribute to the church rather than saving their soul. Let me clear something up with you. All leaders and church folks are not like this, but I can tell you about what I have been through and what I have witness others go through.

When your abused spiritually, mentally, emotionally and sexually you will know by how your spirit feels when it happens to you. When a person have been abused and deprived, it make you feel insignificant instead of feeling like your counted as one of Gods Kingdom builders. Spiritual abuse for me was the most hurtful, but in many ways helpful, because it equipped and elevated me spiritually. Yes physical abuse is bad; but there is something about spiritual abuse when leaders and church folks who say that they are Christians and represent the love of Christ; slap you in the face, talk behind your back, lie on you, create rumors and be quick to judge who you say God has called you to be. I have been under leadership (pastors) who have put me on the back burner because of my gifts and the anointing that rest upon my life. I was able to serve at my own church but when visiting churches came or we was invited to be on program at another church. I was set down while others went forth because of the fear of someone seeing the anointing that saturates me. I was to keep silent and be used for their own personal benefit. Some of the leaders I have been under did not care about my soul. They cared about keeping me for themselves to be counted as another number to build their vision. It is nothing wrong with helping your pastor build his or her ministry, you are suppose to build on to the Kingdom of God. How can you build on your vision, if you will not help build someone else vision. I have been told by leaders and church folks that I will never be more anointed than them, even though I never told them that I was. I have been told that my ministry was going to fail in order to discourage me. I have had church folks (women) put me in competitions that I did not know I was in. I thought we all was here to put our gifts together to operate as one for the Kingdom of God. I have came across a couple of elderly women that have been in this thing a long time, roll their eyes at me, smack their lips and fold their arms as if their generation is the only one that God uses. I have been thrown in battles between church clicks without even knowing it. I know what it is like to present ideas to the church committee for an event and so called church folks look down on me and then ran off with the idea and took it as their own giving themselves the credit and glory. I know what it is like to be counted out of meetings because of church folks dealing with the spirit of intimidation and jealousy. I have dealt with the me, myself and I folks that want to make everyone think that they did everything themselves without the help of other saints in the church. I took the abuse, swallowed it, set back and said nothing. God allow us to encounter certain situations but his plan is for good and not for evil. There are lessons to be learned out of these kinds of situations. Whether it is patients, learning to serve and love inspite of. Whether it's learning to forgive. Whether it's learning to overcome the spirit of offense and retaliation. Whether it's learning to deal with emotions. Whether it's learning to hold our tongue. whether it's learning how to serve and love inspite of.

## *Spiritual Food for Thought*

*2 Timothy 2:4 states: 4. No man that warreth entangleth himself with the affairs of this life; that he may please him who hath chosen him to be a soldier.*

I took the abuse and hardships like a good soldier. Instead of going off and telling them a piece of my mind what God was doing in and through me, he kept me quiet. God began preparing me for what is to come. It seemed like a constant struggle to deliver my spiritual babies because of all the confusion and mess in leaders and church folks. The reason why there is so much confusion and mess in the church is because the Sheppard's are at war within themselves. The congregation is a reflection of its pastor. When the pastor is operating in dysfunction, the church operate in dysfunction. It is like a domino effect. It is also like a disease that root and spread to every part of the body shutting it down and then killing it. When the head is operating in dysfunction the sheep becomes scattered. It is sad when leaders themselves like to be involved in mess and brawls between the sheep of the church. I personally have witnessed pastors being the ringleader of junk and mess causing church folks to walk away from the church.

## Spiritual Food for Thought

**Romans 12:17-21** *states: 17. Recompense to no man evil for evil. Provide things honest in the sight of all men. 18. If it be possible, as much as lieth in you, live peaceably with all men. 19. Dearly beloved, avenge not yourselves; I will repay, saith the Lord. 20. Therefore if thine enemy hunger, feed him; if he thirst, give him drink: for in so doing thou shalt heap coals of fire on his head. 21. Be not overcome of evil, but overcome evil with good.*

## Self Dialog

My biggest mistake was allowing leaders to approach me in a state of vulnerability and I suffered because of it. I have dealt with single pastors and I have also dealt with married pastor that told me him and his wife was separated and they were in the middle of a divorce, only to find out much later that the couple was reconciling. These are messengers of the five fold ministry. I couldn't figure out why ministers of the gospel were the only men approaching me. I could not catch a break from them. Little did I know that the so called men of God had their own hidden agenda's when it came to me. Take heed when someone tell you beware of wolves in sheep clothing. I have set under two leaders and one that I did not sit under scope out my anointing and my body. They preyed on me and used it to their advantage. The leaders that have approached me, lied on God and said God told them, that I was their wife and that I was compatible in every way spiritually and naturally. Even though I have grown to become mature in God and have forgiven them and myself. This is going to hurt me to wright this next part, but I have to in order to help somebody get healed, delivered and set free. I had been caught up in a couple of personal relationships outside of church with leaders of the gospel. I believed in their lies about being their wife and it lead to dating and on occasions sex rather than keeping it holy. We defiled ourselves while in ministry. Let me clarify something. Not all leaders are prowlers, controlling, liars, deceitful and manipulators. There are so many honest leaders that fear the Lord and are after Gods on heart to win souls and push them toward their purpose. In addition, there are many honest and faithful single and married leaders that will not use the word of God to prey on people because of the love and fear God. Before sitting under a leader, make sure that your leader has a covering. Make sure that your leader heart and motives are pure and in good standing with God. If it is in good standing with God, it will be in good standing with you. Let the truth be told, the type of leaders that we sit under tells a lot about us. Ouch I stepped on some toes, even my own. Thank God for deliverance.

## Spiritual Food for Thought

*Proverbs 12:2-3 states: 2. A good man obtaineth favour of the Lord: but a man of wicked devices will he condemn. 3. A man shall not be established by wickedness: but the root of the righteous shall not be moved.*

## Self Dialog

It was all a set up by satan to throw me off course. I was reeled in by manipulation of the word and because of lustful desires the end result was flesh. The pastors was not all to blame. I fell by my own lust that's why I could not see past the imitation. I did not want to see past the whining and dining and the making of future plans for us and the vision of the church. The joke was on me because I was nowhere in their current or future plan. I was only bait. After a while of dating I began to wonder if I was really the one God designed and sent as a wife. Where is the ring? If I am the one, why are we dating in secret? Why is it taking so long for you to marry me, if God said that I am the one? When God ordains it, it's a joyous occasion and he wants us to celebrate openly. When it's God, it is not hidden in the dark behind closed doors. The enemy knows no boundaries and he knows how to dress to impress. The enemy knows how to hold a mature conversation. The enemy knows how to whine and dine. The enemy can dwell in a person and they still preach with power and anointing. I have cried, had headaches and even isolated myself from church or anything to do with church. I felt as if I went to church to be apart of everybody's jokes. The leaders that I have set under knew what was going on with jealous church folks, but said nothing in my defense. They backed me up in private and applaud how strong I was to endure. They liked the way I carried myself in the midst of it all but when it came to rebuking the ones that were against me in public they were silent. My head had been filled with practiced speeches. I say practice speeches because the leaders who strung me along have done this more than once and with more than one woman. I was bait ready to be eaten alive. Leaders that I have been under reeled me in just so I would stay in their ministry because of my gifts. They did not care about the calling on my life. The so called few leaders I have dated have lied on me, cheated on me and left me empty after they drained what they wanted out of me. I am talking spiritual, emotionally, mentally and sexually. I felt as if I could not turn to leaders for help. Where can I go, if I can't go to the church? The elders that I did confide in wanted me to sweep it under the rug and never speak of it again. They was protecting the mess. I could not go to the leaders because they were apart of the problem. I felt used and abused. My spiritual gifts had been robbed. I allowed them to intrude without a fight. I wanted to please people who I know did not have my best interest at heart. I often felt dirty when leaving the church because of the mess that was swept under the rug. I was often tired and fatigued because I was being sucked dry by leaches called leaders and church folks. If it was not my spiritual gift, it was my finances. If it was not my finances, it was my transportation. If it was not my transportation, it was sex or all four. I began questioning God again. I questioned him when I was in the world and now in my saved life. I asks God is this what I am put on earth to do? Was I put here only to be used and abused by folks how ever they see fit? I told God that I did not want to sit under anymore leaders because they were jacked up themselves. I told God to never send another preacher my way to be in a relationship with because I could not take anymore of the spiritual, sexual, mental and emotional abuse. One day God set me down and talked to me. God said "Daughter what is it about you, that they think they have the right to approach you like this?" That hurt when God said that to me. God said he allowed me to go through these situations, because what was in me needed to come out. I longed to be married so I can do some of the things a wife do to her husband, such as, know him. The bible called intimacy (know). Due to what I longed for, my discernment was out of focus. So therefore, I was connected to the wrong spirits. I am going to tell you a little secret. Familiar spirits attract one another. God had to deliver me from my filth and from focusing on marriage and the feel good feeling of intimacy. Marriage is more than intimacy. It's a covenant before God and not to be taken lightly. You have to be best friends and operate in unity in all that you do. God had to do some serious purging, delivering and healing to stop the cycle I kept going round and round in. I had to pray, ask for forgiveness and fast constantly. This was while being so called saved and in the church. It does not do the nation any good, if I cover up or sugar coat the truth. To tell the truth and shame the devil some of you are saved, preaching and claiming Christianity and walking this same valley. This is why I had to expose and tell about me to help somebody get delivered from this. If God did it for me, surely He will do it for you. When I sacrificed, God began to open up my eyes to many hidden agenda's from the saved and unsaved. He opened my eyes to many serpents (men and women) that was on the prowl to hunt me down and kill me spiritually, mentally, emotionally with their venom. Most of all God opened my eyes to me. Now I can see it coming from a far and rebuke it before it attacks. God allowed me to take that whipping only to build me, shape me and mold me. Going through abuse strengthened me in my walk with God. The valley of being pimped and prostituted put me in a position to where I could not go to anybody else but God. I was elevated into a higher realm in God through spiritual abuse. It pushed me to purpose. What was meant to hurt and break me built me. When I reflect on what I have been through. I thank God because if I had not gone through what I went through, I would not be where I am today. I was pimped and prostituted spiritually, mentally, emotionally and sexually. What I went through did not feel good nor look good; but through it all, a lesson was learned and the tests was passed after failing many times. I had to learn that everybody that say they like you, have your back or say that your anointed is not your friend. Some people are on assignment by the devil just to be an obstacle in order to hinder your purpose. This is why we should be careful in who we entertain.

# CHAPTER FOURTEEN

## *The Valley of the Brick Wall That*

## *Would Not Move*

## *(Tired and Fatigued)*

### Spiritual Food for Thought

**Romans 6:14-23** *states: 14. For sin shall not have dominion over you: for ye are not under the law, but under grace. 15. What then? Shall we sin, because we are not under the law, but under grace? God forbid. 16. Know ye not, that to whom ye yield yourselves servants to obey, his servants ye are to whom ye obey; whether of sin unto death, or of obedience unto righteousness? 17. But God be thanked, that ye were the servants of sin, but ye have obeyed from the heart that form of doctrine which was delivered you. 18. Being then made free from sin, ye became the servants of righteousness. 19. I speak after the manner of men because of the infirmity of your flesh: for as ye have yielded your members servants to uncleanness and to iniquity unto iniquity; even so now* *yield your members servants to righteousness unto holiness. 20. For when ye were the servants of sin, ye were free from righteousness. 21. What fruit had ye then in those things whereof ye are now ashamed? For the end of those things is death. 22. But now being made free from sin, and become servants to God, ye have your fruit unto holiness, and the end everlasting life. 23. For the wages of sin is death; but the gift of God is eternal life through Jesus Christ our Lord.*

**The definition of Tired**: Is when one is exhausted of strength or energy; fatigued.

**The definition of a Dead End**: Means the end of something.

## Self Dialog

When facing a brick wall you cannot go through it. You cannot go over it. You cannot go around it nor go underneath it. There are restrictions that prevent you from moving forward when facing a brick wall. A brick wall will make you stand still, evaluate something's and force you to take a different approach or another route.

My life was messy and unorganized. Everything I did went wrong. Everything I had worked for dissolved little by little. I lost my job and the money I had saved was leaving quicker than it had come. I came into realization that I found myself always starting over. For the life of me in some areas, I just could not get it together. I kept finding myself in unstable positions. My family stepped in to rescue me time after time again. I was confused, tired, fatigued and frustrated because it seemed like the more I tried or the more steps I took forward, I got knocked back five. I went searching for where i went wrong in life. I realized, that when I started a project, I never finished because of situations that I allowed to block or hinder the progress. For many nights I tossed and turned with insomnia (lack of sleep). I was at a stand still in my life. I was getting nowhere. My mind, body and soul kept hitting a brick wall, as if it was going to move out of my way on it's on free will. When I went left, the brick was there. When I went to the right, the brick was there. I wanted to experience joy, be happy and live a peaceful life; but I had not yet given up the things that it took to get me there. My own will had me bound and locked up in a spiritual prison cell alone and in the dark. I struggled with warfare. I felt as if the weight of the world had crashed in on me. I felt smothered as if I was being suffocated drowning in my own space. I went looking for help from family and friends but no one would answer and come to my aid. I searched for places to get government assistance, but could not find relief. The brick wall stood firm and would not move. My life was like a maze. I went into the maze blind hoping to find my way out. I could have been nominated for the crash course in life award if there was such award ceremony. My intentions was to put myself in drive and move forward; But somehow my gears always shifted in reverse or neutral. The revelation was that I put my own self in the drivers seat and did not allow God to drive and take me where I needed to go. Isn't God the one that know which highway I should travel on because He was the one who created my destiny? Isn't God the one that knows what streets to take and which ones not take? Isn't God the one that knows what areas in life are under construction? Isn't God the one that knows which exit to take? Why didn't I let God drive? The zeal was there but I would allow myself to fall short of arriving to my destination. My spirit man was spiritually dehydrated. My spirit man was parched with thirst waiting to be quenched from an ongoing drought. I got up from off my bed, closed the door, pulled out my notepad, made a checklist and evaluated myself. When I evaluated myself, I discovered that I did not like what I had seen on paper. What I saw in myself was ugly, unclean and it stunk bad. I dealt with some inner issues that kept myself from moving forward towards my future. I looked at my notepad and realized that I was the one getting in my own way from the decisions I had made in life. What I saw was a woman that was empty, scared, rejected and feeling like I had a bunch of promises that would not be fulfilled. What I saw was a woman that was tired of going through the same old cycle year in and year out. What I saw was a woman that had handcuffed her own self. I was headed for self destruction. I hit the brick wall, time after time again, going into it full force. I reached the point of having little strength to do anything. All I needed to do was hit that brick wall one more time and that would have been it for me. I had been through a path of suffering. Some of my sufferings was voluntarily and some involuntarily. I soaked my clothes with many tears because of what I had done to myself. I looked up at the mirror that stirred me directly in my face and saw that the woman in the mirror was my own worst enemy. I went into shut down mode from the pain of hitting the *"brick wall that would not move."* A lot of my downfalls had come from holding on to stuff that had happened to me. I discovered that I was healed in some areas but not healed completely as a whole. I suppressed much of what had happened to me. My life experiences planted a seed and it grew roots within me. My heart grieved with tears and heaviness. This was not a regular cry that came out. I screamed from the inside out longing for help, for love, for security and for freedom. I did not have the strength to fight this thing by myself anymore. My heart, body and soul could not take anymore of the brutal piercings that life had thrown at me. I was like an unequipped fisherman trying to catch fish without bate or a net; but I still expected good results. My mind grew tired and my mind was clouded with fatigue. I had enough and needed to get spiritually well. For a long time, I had been dealing with a spiritual disease. I was infected with HIV (**Hell Infected Virus**). I allowed spiritual parasites (worldly things) in my spirit. In doing so the parasites went deep, found a home within me and released it's poison causing me to operate in dysfunction. The intention of the poison was to take over my spirit and kill me in my sin. I could not fight off the spiritual infection because there was a lack of spiritual medication (the word of God). There was nothing to dissolve the spiritual parasites that had taken root; so therefore, I was unable to heal and find deliverance. I was a dead man walking. I was spiritually dead because my life was not committed to Christ and Christ is life. I was choking and dying in my own sins. I was looking good on the outside but realized if I was dissected and examined closely, there would be all types of spiritual fungus found within me. I felt like I had to take the initiative and move because God was not moving fast enough for me. I took charge of the steering wheel only to find a dead end. I caught myself staring and looking at this brick wall that stood solid before me. I was trying to find answers in something that could not talk back to me. I would put on my happy face on in front of people as though everything was joyous and all right in my life, when really it hurt to smile. I had gotten tired of carrying around bags of sin that weighed me down. The bags of sin felt as if it outweighed the capacity of my natural body. I could not think straight. My focus was off and my zeal was strained. I grew tired of waking up with headaches and feeling frustrated. I consulted in natural food as a comforting source. My spirit man was in a tug-a-war going back and forth. The pain became so intense from the tug it became unbearable. It was if I had no control over my own life. I went into the direction of strange instructions. My grandmother had a saying "Child your running around here like a chicken with it's head cut off." This mean that one is clueless with no sense of direction. After evaluation I looked down at my blouse and saw that it was soaked full of tears. I thought aloud to myself. How did I let my life escalate to a dead end point? How did I keep running, only to end up going nowhere? How did I keep bumping my head time after time again? How did I ignore the pain from within that was caused by sin? I finally had come to my senses that the things of this world did not love me back. I finally figured out, that I put so much time into seeking people, places and things that could not talk to me, comfort me or love me the way that God can. I shouted aloud amongst myself "WHAT AM I DOING.......lust do not love me, I love it. Drinking do not oblige in me, I oblige in it. The club did not pursue me, I pursued it bumping and grinning to music that did not feel me, I felt it. The material things I possessed I valued, but I was not of value to it. The twisted so called relationships that took so much of my time and energy in being loving, genuine, compassionate and understanding did not mean anything to them because it returned back to me void." I covered my heart with my right hand while gasping for breath from dwelling in ignorance. I wasted many years of running into a dead end. It seemed as if everybody around me was prospering, arriving and doing well; while I fell short and suffered. It seemed as if everyone around me was happy and married while I set in sorrow and loneliness. My well had run dry. I felt like I could not get a pinch of water to save my life. I found myself in a dry place. I decided that I wanted to see some positive results. I wanted to see the finish line so I decided to turn my life around or either get left behind. I ask God to shelter me away from myself. I had to reverse the very thing the devil told me I could not have and that was a peace of mind. I knew the visions and dreams that God had planted inside of me. I went and revisited those visions and dreams that needed to come to life. However, in order to give it life, I first needed life restored into me. I wanted and needed to be revived, renewed and restored. I wanted and needed to be shaken up and made over from the inside out. I was incomplete. I wanted and needed to be complete. I turned away from the mirror that showed me all of my stagnation and questioned myself. How can I perform a task when I was not ready to handle it? How can the spiritually dead bring something to life? The dead cannot resurrect the dead. I said I loved God but my actions showed otherwise. I had gotten it now. God allowed me to encounter certain circumstances in order to show me who I really was and where I stood in Him. I knew I had a choice to draw to God voluntarily, but I chose the long way around and had to come in involuntarily with my heart weak and hands up. I buckled, gave in, fell to my knees, ask God to arrest me and take me into custody. I became still and God spoke. God began speaking to me in the most gentle and soothing voice in such a way a father with compassion speaks to his daughter. God told me that I had to go through the storms of life in order to surrender to Him totally. It was then I learned how to trust, lean and depend on God alone. Going through the storms in the valley made me reach out to Him for there was no other help. I apologized to God and then forgave myself for acting careless. I told God, that the poison (sin) that I let effect my life was at the breaking point of tarring me apart. I told God that being the classy woman that I am. I was at war within myself. I asks God to penetrate me with holiness and righteousness. I asks God to purge out every demonic spirit that had a hold on me. I asks God to circumcise my heart from the access weight of sin that was too heavy to bare. I asks God to fill the voided spaces in my life with His presence. I asks God to wash away the old, so I can become new. I was thirsty for this man called Jesus that had come to my rescue time after time again. I wanted a closer walk and talk with thee. Whatever it took to get Him and keep Him I was ready to yield to it. I had enough of playing around with the devil and the devil playing around with me. I had done so much to please the ways of the enemy and in return got a beat down.

## Spiritual Food for Thought

**Psalms 42:1** *states: 1. As the heart panteth after the water brooks, so panteth my soul after thee, O God.*

## Self Dialog

I was on the hunt for this man named Jesus who had been there this whole time. He was there and welcomed me warmly as if I had been faithful to Him. From that day on, I learned to draw a line of scrimmage between the devil and myself. Do you remember back in the day when a fight was about to break out, you knew when someone was serious. When a person felt like they could not be defeated by his or her opponent they would bend down and draw a line between them and their opponent and dared them if they were big, bad and bold enough to cross the line. This was a sign that a beat down was coming if you crossed that line. I began to apply that theory to my own life against the devil. I became bold and made up in my mind that I was going to stand toe to toe with the devil. I drew that line of scrimmage in my life against the devil. I had to let the devil know, that I was prepared and I was coming equipped and empowered. I said this time, I was ready to fight for my life and that of my loved ones. I let the devil know, that I worked too hard and had come too far to let him take whatever he wanted without a fight. The devil had taken stuff from me for years and I was not about to let it happen again. I told the devil you do not run me anymore I run you. I had to muster up a bulldog fight in the spiritual realm against the devil. I could no longer fight the devil with the mindset of a poodle. The poodle mentality was the reason I was getting beat up so much by the enemy. I got mad and told the devil off and this is exactly how I talked to him. "If you are thinking about coming across this line to come in between God and I. THE FIGHT IS ON!" I told the devil. "If you are thinking about crossing this line to attack my family. YOU BETTER WATCH OUT BECAUSE YOUR ABOUT TO GO DOWN!" "If you are thinking about crossing this line to attack my visions and dreams. WATCH OUT BECAUSE A TKO IS COMING BECAUSE THE VICTORY IS MINE!" I told the devil. "If you are thinking about attacking whatever belongs to me period, whether spiritual or natural. I AM GOING TO SLICE AND DICE YOU WITH THE WORD OF GOD BECAUSE THAT IS MY WEAPON!" I told the devil. "If you are thinking about crossing this line to attack my finances. I WILL DROP YOU WITH THE ANOINTING THAT IS ON MY LIFE!" I told the devil. "CROSS THIS LINE IF YOU WANT TO. I WILL HUFF, I WILL PUFF AND I WILL BLOW YOUR KINGDOM DOWN!" I told the devil. "THE GOD THAT IS NOW IN ME WILL NOT AND SHALL NOT STAND FOR ANYTHING!" I literally had to act as if I had lost my mind in order for the devil to back up off of me. I made a decision to stand on my post and not be moved. I told the devil. "YOU CAN SET THE TRAP, BUT IT WILL BE FOUND AND DESTROYED!" I told the devil. "YOU CAN FORM THE WEAPON, BUT IT WILL BACK FIRE!" I told the devil. "YOU CAN DIG THE DITCH, BUT YOU WILL BE THE

ONE TO FALL IN IT!" I had it now. The reason the devil was able to approach me so easily because my routine was the same. I went about my daily business as usual, day in and day out. The devil is a sneaky and conniving snake and he is out to bate in, poison and kill. I had to put on a bulldog mentality against the devil. A bulldog is vicious and if you approach it the wrong way they will attack you and bite you with no intentions on letting go until they see blood. I had to learn I could not fight him in the natural that is why I grew tired, fatigued and at a dead end. I was going about the strategy the wrong way. I left out the most important weapon and his name is Jesus. I had to go back and get my help. I turned my battles over to God. I was not created to be walked on, abuse and misused to only end up at a dead end. I was not put here on earth to give into the devil, so I can whither and die in his camp. I was not put here on earth to serve the devil and go through all types of hurt and painful things, die, open my eyes up in hell just to go through some more hell. Oh, somebody did not catch that! I decided to go back to church. I wanted to get acquainted on how to do things and get in the midst of love. I wanted to be where I could be fed and filled with the Holy Ghost fire that everyone talked about. I wanted to have a for real and personal encounter with God. I wanted him to touch me. I wanted to know what it was like to be in His presence for real. I needed God more now than I ever have before. I could not think or breathe without Him. I could not operate daily and be productive without Him. I needed to know that God was near me at all times. I wanted to know this man name Jesus whom the people spoke of that ordered their steps. I was done playing hide and seek and pick a boo. I wanted God to catch me, tag me and say servant your it. I was willing to go and do whatever it took in order for me to move forward. I had gotten my zeal back. I found my real first love. I embraced Him and He embraced me and I was not about to let Him go. I was at the age of 27 years old. I had matured and I knew who I wanted and that was God and everything He has for me. I resembled the protocol son that went astray; but when I came home, Jesus received me with open arms and rejoiced. God did not judge me. God took me and scrapped and scrubbed off all of that stuck on filth that was on me. It is something about when you find your way home to daddy (Jesus) so much peace comes over you. It is time to draw that line in your own life. The only reason why the devil tampered or is tampering with your stuff so much, is because of what you are ordained and anointed to do. However, because you have inherited a coward (poodle) mentality, somewhere along the way it allowed you to bow down and accept anything. God did not put us here to be trampled over by the devil. God our daddy, our overseer, our provider our counselor, our healer and deliverer was the one who gave us the power to conquer the devil and his employees (demons). We have the power to tread over serpents and scorpions. I come to inform you that you did not lose the power that God has given you to defeat the enemy. Somewhere along the way you just put it down and it is waiting for you to return to pick it up again. You are dangerous in the spirit and the devil knows that you are. The devil do not know your ending. The only thing the devil knows to do is to put stumbling blocks in your way to trip you up hoping that the block he put down was the right one to stop you. Keep this in mind that God is the one that gives the devil permission to mess with you. The reason God do this is to let the devil know that no matter what tricks he pull out, it will not work because He has His hand on you. The Lord allowed you to go through somethings because He knows that He is capable of bringing you out. The Lord will never put more on you than you can bare. Speak to your life with the word of God and the power that He has given you and watch what happens. Speak to the wall and it will move on your command.

# CHAPTER FIFTEEN

## *Out of The Valley*

## *Forgive Yourself, Forgive Others and Move On*

### *Self Dialog*

I chose to be disobedient to God and jumped ahead of Him by getting out of His will and into my own will. I had to pay a very high price for the decisions I had made in life. When God did not ordain a person, place or thing to be apart of your destiny, you will suffer the consequences. When God speaks to us sometimes He will tell us "No." It's not because He do not understand or He is too hard. It's because He loves us. God tells us "No" sometimes to keep us from self destruction. Some of our falls come from a hard head and because of that we proceed without clearance.

### *Spiritual Food for Thought*

***James 1: 2-5*** *states: My brethren, count it all joy when ye fall into divers temptations; 3. Knowing this, that the* *trying of your faith worketh patience. 4. But let patience have her perfect work, that ye may be perfect and entire, wanting nothing. 5. If any of you lack wisdom, let him ask of God, that giveth to all men liberally, and upbraideth not; and it shall be given him.*

## Self Dialog

I went through these trials to learn how to stand, be strong and endure. Through it all, I have learned to be patient and humble. I also had to go through humiliation in order to recognize that there is only one God and He is a jealous God that do not want any person, place or thing before Him. The trials and tribulations that we go through in life come to make us and build us up, if we allow it. If I had not gone through what I went through. Would I have surrendered to God? If I had not gone through trials and tribulations. Would my faith and trust be where it is in God? If I had not gone through the *"Valley of the Shadow of death"* experiences. Would I have l learned how to love, hold my tongue and forgive? So I tell you, count it all joy for every trial you have gone through for it has laid a foundation so you can stand firm in knowing who you are and where your going in Christ Jesus.

## Spiritual Food for Thought

*Luke 6:27-28 states: But I say unto you which Hear, Love your enemies, do good to them which hate you. 28. Bless them that curse you, and pray for them which despitefully use you.*

## Self Dialog

The scripture above is stating that REGARDLESS OF WHAT THEY SAY OR DO, BLESS YOUR ENEMIES. Jesus was not always liked, smiled at, encouraged or patted on the back. He was persecuted, wounded, abused and misused by people (flesh). The one thing I love about Jesus inspite of what they had done, He forgave them. Jesus said something so powerful and profound that gave us a perfect example on what to do when people mistreat us. Jesus himself forgave and interceded for those who mistreated Him. Jesus made this statement. "Father, forgive them for they not know what they do." REGARDLESS OF WHAT THEY SAY OR DO. FORGIVE AND BLESS YOUR ENEMIES.

## Spiritual Food for Thought

*Philippians 3:14 states: 13. Brethren, I count not myself to have apprehended: but the one thing I do, forgetting those things which are behind, and reaching forth unto those things which are before. 14. I press towards the mark for the prize of the high calling of God in Christ Jesus.*

## Spiritual Food for Thought

*Matthew 22:23 states: 32. I am the God of Abraham, and the God of Isaac, and the God of Jacob? God is not the God of the dead, but of the living.*

## Self Dialog

You have to forgive yourself. So many times we beat ourselves up over what happened in life. Unforgiveness is one of the number one cause of sickness and death. We all make mistakes and we all have falling short of the glory. You cannot continue this way. You have to forgive yourself and others who have hurt and misused you. Your story is a testimony. You have to forgive.

Think on this. How many times have people had to forgive you? I have one even better. How many times have Jesus had to forgive you? Who are we to hold forgiveness from ourselves and others. Jesus said He threw our sins into the sea of forgiveness to remember them no more. If He can forgive, so can you. There is so much more to you. There are somethings that God want you to tap into, that you did not know was there. In order to operate and receive all that God has for you, you must forgive and choose not to waddle in it another day. When forgiveness takes place in the spirit then you can move on because you chose to take the handcuffs and the shackles off. You can move forward now because you chose to take the limits off yourself and God. Moving on feels good. Moving on means that you are free to operate. Your free to think clearly. Your free to praise and worship. Your heart is free to receive and birth out what God has imparted into you. When God is in it, your free to move on in your family, free to move on in your relationships spiritual and natural without demonic influence. The decision to move on mean that you have picked up your bed and decided to walk. You have made the decision to pick up your bed and walk. You have made the decision to not die but live. You have made the decision to break generational curses. You have chosen to dwell in peace, love, joy and happiness. The decision to forgive and move on mean that your spirit man have traded in bondage for salvation, healing, deliverance, miracles, signs and wonders. The decision to move on mean no more hinderance, no more hesitation, no more brick walls and no more death sentences from the devil. The decision to forgive and move on have allowed you to tell that assassination spirit called Jezebel, Cain, Haman and Delilah to be thou removed because you are moving on in Jesus name! Move on, live and eat the bread of life (the word of God). Oh, taste and see that the Lord is good. The water from the well is flowing. So drink from the water that never runs dry. Now smile soldier for you have been set free. You have been equipped and suited up and ready for battle. You have been given instruction by way of the Holy Ghost on what to do. You have encountered, went through and made it out. Now go soldier and go with a clean heart, a new spirit, zeal, grace, boldness, humbleness, love and gladness. Walk in the authority for you have found **"LIFE, THOUGH YOU WALKED THROUGH THE VALLEY OF THE SHADOW OF DEATH."** God bless you and the words of our LORD and SAVIOR JESUS CHRIST.

# "IT IS FINISHED"

# ABOUT THE AUTHOR

*Seer, Evangelist, Prayer Warrior, Revivalist, Co-Pastor, Motivational Speaker, Mentor, Entrepreneur and Author*

I am 36 years of age and currently reside in Dallas, Texas. I graduated from South University in Savannah, Georgia, where I've received my Associates Degree in Business Administration. I am the wife of Apostle J.L Clarkson he is the CEO/Founder of Ministry of Sonship. I am a proud mother of 3 boys Domadrick, Marquavous & Jermaine Jr. They are truly God's gift to me. The mantle that I carry and the anointing that is on my life requires me to push full force. Since January 2010, God spoke to me about the name of the ministries He wanted me to birth forth. The name of the ministries are ( SCMinistries/Just One Drop of his Blood Ministries) where I am the Founder and Overseer. This ministry is an outside of the four walls ministry. God has been dealing with me a long time about my calling. I had to surrender and trust God to operate in me. As of March 22, 2010. I accepted my true calling in the 5 fold ministry as Seer going about the nation, doing Evangelist work. This ministry is about going about our Father's business in revival going from city to city, state to state and country to country with the help of our Lord and Savior Jesus Christ. We come in the name of our Lord and Savior Jesus Christ to equip and to empower the nation by bringing the nations out of Egypt (a bound place) by preaching the gospel of Jesus Christ, laboring in much prayer and fasting that results in healing and deliverance. I am the author of 'Life, Though I Walked Through the Valley of the Shadow of Death.' This book was inspired and birthed through my real life story. This book is about the storms I have gone through and what I did to keep my sanity while enduring these valley experiences. This book is about how I went through the valley and how I made it out. Now that the valley is over. What's next? Where do I go from here? This is a christian based book with biblical teachings from the KJV bible. This book will strengthen and give hope to Gods people. This book will bring forth healing, deliverance, salvation forgiveness, repentance and most of all a closer relationship with Jesus.

Made in the USA
Middletown, DE
14 November 2022

14992696R00096